THE NATURAL
vegan
kitchen

Recipes from the
Natural Kitchen
Cooking School

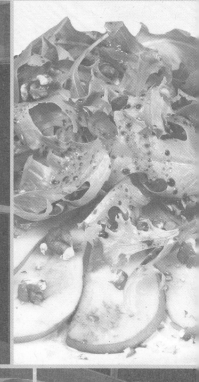

CHRISTINE WALTERMYER

Cover design: John Wincek
Interior design: Jim Scattaregia
Interior photos: Warren Jefferson
Food styling: Barbara Jefferson

Book Publishing Company
P.O. Box 99
Summertown, TN 38483
888-260-8458
www.bookpubco.com

ISBN: 978-1-57067-245-3

Printed in Canada

17 16 15 14 13 12 11   9 8 7 6 5 4 3 2 1

Library of Congress Cataloging-in-Publication Data
Waltermyer, Christine.
 The natural vegan kitchen : recipes from the Natural Kitchen Cooking School / Christine Waltermyer.
     p. cm.
 Includes index.
 ISBN 978-1-57067-245-3
 1. Vegan cooking. 2. Cookbooks. I. Natural Kitchen Cooking School. II. Title.
 TX837.W273 2010
 641.5'636--dc22

                    2010035559

Printed on recycled paper

Book Publishing Company is a member of Green Press Initiative. We chose to print this title on paper with 100% postconsumer recycled content, processed without chlorine, which save the following natural resources:

80 trees
2,237 pounds of solid waste
36,845 gallons of water
7,650 pounds of greenhouse gases
25 million BTU of energy

For more information on Green Press Initiative, visit www.greenpressinitiative.org. Environmental impact estimates were made using the Environmental Defense Fund Paper Calculator. For more information visit www.papercalculator.org.

Contents

FOR MY BEAUTIFUL DAUGHTER, ANYA.
You are the gift of my life, and I love you with everything.

Foreword

I USED TO EAT AT BURGER KING SEVEN DAYS A WEEK. (Bacon double-cheeseburger, small fries, and a small Coke was my standard order.) I ate meat at every meal. I was the girl who took the cheese and pepperoni friends discarded from their pizzas and put it on my own. To say I was a "bad eater" would be an understatement. Not surprisingly, my mood, health, and energy level reflected my poor diet.

I became a vegetarian in 1994, after learning about factory farming and slaughterhouses. How could I call myself an animal lover while contributing to the torture and slaughter of animals? I changed my ways overnight. And I hated it. I remember crying in a restaurant during my first week as a vegetarian; there was not one single thing I wanted on the menu—except meat. But my compassion for animals kept my eating habits honest. And now, seventeen years later, not only do I love food more than ever, I also can appreciate how beneficial a veg diet is for my health and for the planet. I'm happier, healthier, and in better shape now than I was as a teenager—and I owe it all to my vegan diet. But it's a shame that my early days as a compassionate, conscientious consumer were spent in such misery. I had no idea how amazing veggie food could be.

If only I had met Christine Waltermyer way back then. Food coach, health counselor, chef, cooking instructor—she is a culinary *machine*. For many, eating is the most pleasurable activity in the world, and no one understands this better than Christine. She fully gets that in order for people to even slightly adjust their diets, the food has to be outstanding. Every meal has to induce a "food-gasmic" experience or there's just no point in eating. At the same time, we need to take care of our precious health. That's the beauty of what Christine creates: amazing food that is out of this world yet good for you. "Healthy pleasures" need not be an oxymoron; with Christine's recipes, we can have our cake *and* eat it. Christine's thorough knowledge of nutrition, paired with her exceptional culinary ability, is what makes her so good at what she does.

Whether you're veg, vegan, meat-centric, somewhere in between, or just looking to change things up a little, *The Natural Vegan Kitchen* will knock your socks off. It will awaken your taste buds and retrain them to appreciate delicious, wholesome food. It will inspire you to eat the way you were meant to. And most important of all, it will induce multiple "food-gasms."

—**Rory Freedman**, coauthor, *Skinny Bitch*

Acknowledgments

I OWE HUGE THANKS TO ALL OF YOU WHO MADE THIS BOOK POSSIBLE. Thank you, Mom and Dad, for your tremendous love and support. Mom, you've always been my confidant, my inspiration, and my first and greatest cooking teacher. Thank you, Dad, for the walks, the motorcycle rides, your admirable work ethic, and your appreciation of the natural world. To my sister, Cathy, and her family, Mark, Ben, Hannah, and Abby, thank you for your love and all of the fun we always have together. Thanks, Chuck, for all of our adventures and great meals together. Peter, I can't thank you enough for how you've blessed my life.

I would also like to thank Cynthia Holzapfel, Jo Stepaniak, Anna Pope, and everyone at Book Publishing Company for being so great to work with and for helping to bring this book to fruition. Very special thanks to Mary Flynn and Joyce Rosenblum, without whom the Natural Kitchen Cooking School would not be where it is today. Zillions of thanks to supporters of my cooking classes over the years, including Dean Nelson, David Weigel, and all of the staff at Dean's Natural Food Market; Kat and Frank Grausso; Johanna Schwarzbeck and Egon Zippel, as well as Melissa McDermott, Tricia Rago, Nirit Yadin, Christine Carroll, Wai Chu, Min Liao, and everyone at the Whole Foods Market in Princeton, New Jersey, and the Whole Foods Market Bowery in New York City. You have all been truly amazing to work with! Thank you to all of the incredible assistants, students, and clients of the Natural Kitchen Cooking School over the years. Huge thanks to the Littenberg family, who taught me so much and helped me to realize which recipes were the real gems. I cherish all of my wonderful friends and girl buddies over the years. You know who you are!

I would never have known anything about healthful cooking if it were not for Michio and Aveline Kushi and the natural-food movement they created here in the United States. Rory Freedman and Christina Pirello are two of my superheroines, and I am in awe of them both. Thank you to all of the other incredible individuals who have inspired me along the way, including Osho, Eckhardt Tolle, Byron Katie, Howard Lyman, Madonna, John Robbins, Luchi Barnda, and Joshua Rosenthal. Thank you to Neal Barnard, MD, Jill Eckhardt, and Mary and Peter Max for your generous support of this book. Special thanks to the gifted Robin Robertson, whose expertise and advice was invaluable in the process of writing my first cookbook. Peter, I can't thank you enough for the blessing of sweet Anya.

Finally, I am grateful to the animal companions who have been in my life, for loving me unconditionally.

Preface
The Journey

A journey of a thousand miles begins with a single step.
—**Lao-tzu**, *The Way of Lao-tzu*

SINCE PUBERTY MY BOOBS HAD BECOME FIBROID FACTORIES, producing ridiculous amounts of annoying, uncomfortable, hard lumps, each of which I was told could grow to the size of grapefruits. After two surgeries, with twenty lumps removed and at least that many sprouting up in their place, my doctor suggested a double mastectomy. Hmm . . . radical, disfiguring surgery at the age of twenty-two for a benign condition? I don't think so. I would find an alternative.

My quest began on Thanksgiving Day, 1992. I decided to forgo the turkey that day and never have it again. I was going vegetarian, and it felt right. This was the first step of my journey. I began exploring the world of alternative health, taking programs at the Omega Institute for Holistic Studies in Rhinebeck, New York, and studying yoga at the Kripalu Center for Yoga & Health in Stockbridge, Massachusetts. I started hiking, stretching, meditating, sleeping outside in a tent under the stars, and yelling (nothing like a little primal therapy for what ails you). It felt amazing. I transformed into a calmer, saner, happier person, and the boobs were intact.

When I first stopped eating meat, I was the epitome of a junk-food vegetarian. *Hydrox cookies are vegan? Great! Bring 'em on—in buckets!* Step two of my journey was discovering macrobiotic food at the Kushi Institute in Becket, Massachusetts. My first macrobiotic meal there consisted of whole-grain brown rice, kale, and beans, and it was an epiphany. The food was no-frills simple, yet it tasted like manna from heaven. I remember chewing, and chewing, and chewing

. . . and hearing miraculous stories from people sitting next to me at dinner. One guy was in remission from what was considered terminal cancer, and it happened just by his changing what he ate. I thought *Why isn't this front page news? Why don't more young women facing double mastectomies know about this?* I decided I was going to tell the whole world.

I had always wanted to somehow help people, animals, and the environment, and have a blast and be creative while doing so. The moment of my epiphany came when I realized I could tie all of these aspirations together by teaching natural-food cooking. That day at the Kushi Institute, while I was chewing on that sweet brown rice, my destiny unfolded before me. I was going to transform the world, armed with carrots, kale, and barley. It was time to don my apron, take up my chef's knife, and become the health crusader I was born to be! I knew it was going to be delicious journey.

A few years later, and with many veggie meals under my belt, the life of my dreams has materialized. I started a cooking school and work with people I adore. I feel healthier than ever. Because of my diet and lifestyle changes, the boob lumps stopped growing and are no longer a problem. In addition, I've become a total yoga junkie and feel a level of calm and contentment I never thought possible.

I love it when everybody wins. The recipes in *The Natural Vegan Cooking* are not only tasty, they're good for you, good for the animals, and good for the planet. So what are you waiting for? Take the first step of *your* journey. Don that funky apron, grab a knife, and bring a fork!

natural vegan kitchen
The Way of the Natural Vegan Kitchen

ONE OF THE BEST COMPLIMENTS I'VE EVER RECEIVED came from a student in one of my cooking classes who was new to healthful cooking. As he sat in his chair munching on a veggie burger I had made, he suddenly blurted out, "This tastes like it's *bad* for you!" I gave myself an inner high five with a resounding *Yes!*

For a health-promoting diet to last a lifetime, the food has to taste so good we think it must be bad for us. Otherwise, why bother. That's why I started the Natural Kitchen Cooking School and developed the recipes for *The Natural Vegan Kitchen*. In this book you'll find recipes that are luscious, satisfying, and full of familiar flavors. Although I'd like to claim that this way of eating is something totally new that I invented, I actually swiped the idea from my ancestors (and yours too), who, back in the day, ate whole, unrefined foods grown without pesticides and other chemicals—long before eating organic food was considered hip.

In just the last sixty years, how our food is grown and prepared has changed dramatically. Even as recently as our grandparents' time, "slow food" was how everyone ate. There were no microwave ovens, neon blue breakfast cereals, or fast-food triple-mega burgers. There also were no factory farms, growth hormones, GMOs, artificial flavors, artificial colors, or preservatives. We're among the first generations to be formula fed, vaccinated, and subsisting on a steady diet of processed foods laden with fat, sugar, and salt. Americans as a group

A Note about Oil

For many of my recipes I use a combination of grapeseed oil and water for sautéing. Although grapeseed oil is not traditionally used in macrobiotic cooking, I prefer it for several reasons. Grapeseed oil can withstand higher temperatures than most other cooking oils, and it is rich in vitamin E, which helps make it a very stable oil. Grapeseed oil contains powerful antioxidants. The mono- and polyunsaturated fats in grapeseed oil help to lower blood pressure. Grapeseed oil is rich in linoleic acid, a heart-healthy omega-6 fatty acid. It has been studied for its ability to maintain healthy cholesterol levels in the body by lowering LDL ("bad" cholesterol) and raising HDL ("good" cholesterol).

Combining grapeseed oil (or any other cooking oil, such as sesame oil) with water will help keep the temperature of the oil lower so you can avoid overheating it. If you prefer to cook without any oil at all, just use water to steam-fry vegetables.

Even though grapeseed oil has so many health benefits, I tend to minimize the use of cooking oils in general because when oils are separated from their source (that is, whole nuts, seeds, or beans), they are more susceptible to rancidity. Instead, I opt for whole foods that are rich in healthful omega-3 fats, such as avocados, ground flaxseeds, hempseeds, and walnuts.

are consuming far more meat, eggs, and dairy products than ever before. All of these factors have contributed to our growing health crisis and have made cancer, diabetes, heart disease, obesity, and stroke—rare ailments in our grandparents' day—commonplace.

The term *macrobiotics* was first used by Hippocrates, the ancient Greek philosopher attributed with being the father of Western medicine. *Macro* means "large," and *bios* means "life." Therefore, the practice of macrobiotics entails the art of prolonging life and living it to its fullest. When I first heard about macrobiotics, this philosophy grabbed my attention and drew me in. The following are some of the key macrobiotic principles for enjoying a long, healthy, and happy life:

1. Eat in harmony with your natural surroundings. Select foods that are in season and grown locally.

2. Maintain balance in your life and diet. Macrobiotics emphasizes the balance of yin and yang, two opposing yet complementary forces of natural energy, such as light and dark or male and female. Yin and yang energies are also present in the foods we eat. Examples of yin foods are alcohol, coffee, sugar, and white flour. Consuming yin foods could lead to feeling sleepy, sad, or "spaced out." Examples of yang foods are baked goods (such as crackers), eggs, hard cheeses, meat, and refined salt. Consuming extremely yang foods could lead to feeling tense, stressed, and angry. Foods that help us feel balanced include organic whole grains (such as brown rice), vegetables, soups, beans, whole-grain noodles, sea vegetables, nuts, seeds, and locally grown fruits. Much has been written on the subject of yin and yang; I encourage you to study these books to understand how to incorporate more balance into your life.

3. Savor mealtimes. Turn off the television, put away the phone, move away from the computer . . . and simply eat. Eating slowly, without distraction, reduces stress, and chewing food thoroughly optimizes digestion, which is essential for good health.

4. Enjoy natural living. Wear clothing made from natural fibers, like cotton and linen. Avoid exposure to electromagnetic radiation, such as through cell phones, X-rays, and microwave ovens. Enjoy a thirty-minute walk every day, and occasionally walk barefoot in the grass. Lightly rub your body from head to toe with a hot towel to clear the pores, discharge toxins, and help the skin to function at optimum efficiency.

The Natural Vegan Kitchen embraces the best of both vegan and macrobiotic diets, encouraging the use of high-quality foods that are as close to their natural state as possible, with nothing added or removed. A standard macrobiotic diet is generally very health-promoting, but the following enhancements will make it even better:

1. Include more raw foods.

2. Supplement with vitamins B_{12} and D_2, the vegan form of vitamin D. (These two nutrients can't be obtained from plant foods.)

3. Avoid eating fish. (Fish are tainted with heavy metals and other contaminants, and fishing is destructive to the environment.)

4. Eat foods rich in omega-3 fatty acids (such as flaxseeds, hempseeds, and walnuts) and supplement with vegan DHA.

5. Reduce or eliminate salt, refined soy products, and foods that contain gluten (see page 15).

6. Include more cultural variety in meals, such as Mexican, Indian, and Italian versions of macrobiotic recipes.

When you opt for foods that are fresh, local, organic, and seasonal, you get more nutritional bang for your buck—more vitamins and minerals and no chemical residues in your body. *The Natural Vegan Kitchen* cooking is the modern way to prepare natural food, which has kept people all over the world in good health since the beginning of civilization.

A Note about Gluten-Free Recipes

Gluten intolerance (celiac disease) and wheat sensitivities are becoming more prevalent. In addition, a growing number of people are avoiding gluten-containing foods (wheat, rye, barley, kamut, and spelt) simply because they feel better when they don't consume them. Oats are generally considered gluten free, but they are commonly contaminated with gluten during farming (by gluten-containing crops), transport (by being shipped in containers also used for wheat-based flour and other gluten-containing foods), and milling (by being processed in facilities that also manufacture gluten-containing products). However, uncontaminated, gluten-free oats are available in natural food stores and from online retailers. Other products that commonly contain gluten—such as tamari, brown rice syrup, tempeh, and vanilla extract—are also available in gluten-free versions. Many of the recipes in this book are gluten free or can be made gluten free, and I have designated them by putting "Gluten Free" beside the recipe titles so you can easily locate them.

CHAPTER TWO

What's for Breakfast?

PEOPLE OFTEN ASK ME WHAT I EAT FOR BREAKFAST; I tell them nails. Just kidding. Actually, I love a wide range of breakfast foods, everything from steel-cut oatmeal with raisins to savory burrito wraps, soups, vegetables, or even noodles. If I prepare a grain porridge, I make sure it's soft and creamy, to ease my digestive system into the day. Topped with ground flaxseeds, walnuts, and fresh or dried fruit, it becomes a breakfast of champions. Miso soup is the classic Japanese breakfast food, and it helps boost energy levels by providing protein and friendly bacteria for strong digestion. Dark green veggies, like kale, have a strong upward growth pattern; eating them is like taking a bite of sunshine. Try some dark leafy greens for breakfast and notice how wonderful you feel.

I have included some familiar breakfast favorites in this chapter to give you nutritious replacements for morning classics. By choosing a nutritious breakfast, you'll feel like a million bucks all day long.

Basic Granola 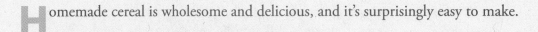 GLUTEN FREE

MAKES 6 CUPS

Homemade cereal is wholesome and delicious, and it's surprisingly easy to make.

4 cups gluten-free rolled oats

½ cup brown rice flour

½ cup gluten-free brown rice syrup

⅓ cup grapeseed oil or other oil

1 teaspoon gluten-free vanilla extract

½ teaspoon ground cinnamon

½ cup chopped walnuts

⅓ cup chopped dried apricots

⅓ cup currants

Preheat the oven to 350 degrees F. Lightly oil a baking sheet.

Combine the oats, flour, syrup, oil, vanilla extract, and cinnamon in a large bowl. Mix thoroughly.

Spread the mixture on the prepared baking sheet. Bake for 10 minutes, or until golden, stirring once halfway through the baking period. Transfer to a bowl to cool, stirring frequently.

When the granola is completely cool, stir in the walnuts, apricots, and currants. Stored in tightly sealed glass jars or storage containers, Basic Granola will keep for 3 weeks at room temperature, 1 month in the refrigerator, or 3 months in the freezer.

Per ¾ cup: calories: 378, protein: 7 g, fat: 16 g, carbohydrate: 46 g, fiber: 5 g, sodium: 7 mg

Sioux Indian Cornmeal Pudding GLUTEN FREE

MAKES 4 SERVINGS

This is a vegan version of a hundred-year-old recipe. Comfort food to the max, this pudding can be served for either breakfast or dessert. For a special treat, top it with a scoop of nondairy ice cream.

3 cups vanilla rice milk

⅓ cup maple syrup

Pinch sea salt

½ teaspoon ground cinnamon

¼ teaspoon ground cardamom

¼ teaspoon ground ginger

½ cup yellow corn grits (polenta)

¼ cup currants

Preheat the oven to 350 degrees F. Lightly oil a 2-quart casserole.

Combine the rice milk, syrup, salt, cinnamon, cardamom, and ginger in a medium saucepan. Bring to a boil over medium-high heat. Slowly add the corn grits, stirring constantly with a whisk to prevent lumping. Stir in the currants. Decrease the heat to low, cover, and cook for 10 minutes, stirring occasionally with a whisk.

Transfer to the prepared casserole. Cover and bake for 20 minutes. Uncover and bake for 10 minutes longer. Serve warm.

Per serving: calories 243, protein: 2 g, fat: 2 g, carbohydrate: 54 g, fiber: 2 g, sodium: 86 mg

French Toast

Thick slabs of French toast, smothered in warm maple syrup . . . what could be better? This low-fat version of a familiar favorite will add a special touch to your breakfast.

2 cups amazake (original, almond, or hazelnut)

1 tablespoon kuzu or arrowroot starch, mixed with ¼ cup cold water

½ teaspoon umeboshi vinegar

2 pinches ground turmeric

8 slices whole-grain bread (slightly stale bread is fine)

1 tablespoon grapeseed oil or other oil

½ teaspoon ground cinnamon

1 cup maple syrup, warmed

Heat a large cast iron skillet over medium heat.

Combine the amazake and kuzu mixture in a large bowl. Add the vinegar and turmeric and whisk until evenly blended. Soak the bread in the mixture for 5 minutes, or until it is well saturated.

Brush the skillet with some of the oil. Put 3 or 4 slices of the soaked bread in the hot skillet and cook for 3 to 5 minutes on each side, or until golden. Repeat with the remaining oil and bread slices.

To serve, cut each slice in half diagonally, sprinkle with the cinnamon, and drizzle with the syrup.

Per serving: calories: 503, protein: 7 g, fat: 6 g, carbohydrate: 109 g, fiber: 2 g, sodium: 357 mg

Tofu-and-Vegetable Scramble GLUTEN FREE

MAKES 6 SERVINGS

Feel free to mix and match your favorite veggies in this dish. Complement the scramble with a side of whole-grain toast.

1 pound firm tofu, drained

2 tablespoons water

1 tablespoon grapeseed oil or other oil

½ cup diced carrots

½ cup fresh or frozen corn kernels

¼ cup diced celery

¼ cup diced red radishes

¼ cup sliced green beans

½ teaspoon umeboshi vinegar

¼ to ½ teaspoon sea salt

⅛ teaspoon ground turmeric

1 teaspoon dried dill weed or other dried herb of choice

2 teaspoons kuzu or arrow root starch, mixed with ¼ cup cold water

Put the tofu in a colander in the sink and put a few small plates on top of it. Let the water drain from the tofu for 10 minutes. Crumble the tofu into a bowl and set aside.

Heat the water and oil in a large skillet or wok over medium-high heat. Add the carrots, corn, celery, radishes, and green beans. Cook and stir for 3 minutes, or until the vegetables have softened but are still bright in color. Put the tofu, vinegar, salt, and turmeric on top of the vegetables. Cover and cook for 5 minutes. Add the dill weed and kuzu mixture and stir until thickened and glossy. Serve hot.

Per serving: calories: 125, protein: 7 g, fat: 7 g, carbohydrate: 7 g, fiber: 2 g, sodium: 102 mg

Power Pancakes `GLUTEN FREE`

MAKES 6 MEDIUM PANCAKES

Mmm . . . a big stack of pancakes smothered in syrup. This version is a gluten-free indulgence to get your day started off right. I serve them drizzled with a combination of brown rice syrup and maple syrup.

Dry Ingredients

1 cup millet flour or other gluten-free flour

1 cup cornmeal

2 teaspoons baking powder

½ teaspoon xanthan gum

⅛ teaspoon sea salt

Wet Ingredients

1 tablespoon grapeseed oil or other oil

2½ cups vanilla rice milk

1 teaspoon brown rice vinegar

Oil for Frying

2 tablespoons grapeseed oil or other oil

Warm a large cast iron skillet or crêpe pan over medium heat while you prepare the pancake batter.

To make the batter, combine the dry ingredients in a large bowl. In a separate small bowl, combine the wet ingredients and mix with a whisk. Add the wet ingredients to the dry ingredients and stir with a whisk until combined. If necessary, add a little more rice milk to achieve a smooth, thick batter.

Lightly brush the skillet with some of the oil and immediately add ¼ cup of batter to form a 3-inch pancake. Add more batter to make 3 or 4 pancakes, or as many as the skillet will hold. After about 3 minutes, when the edges look slightly dry and the surface is covered with bubbles, turn the pancakes over and cook the other side for 3 minutes, or until golden. Keep the pancakes warm in a covered container. Cook the remaining batter in the same manner. Serve hot.

Per pancake: calories: 260, protein: 5 g, fat: 9 g, carbohydrate: 41 g, fiber: 3 g, sodium: 210 mg

Blueberry Pancakes: Add 1 cup of fresh blueberries to the batter, or place the blueberries directly in the pancakes as they cook, so that you can evenly space them.

Pan-Fried Mochi GLUTEN FREE

Mochi gives you something chewy and substantial to sink your teeth into for breakfast. It's made from whole-grain brown rice that has been precooked, so you get all of the benefits of brown rice in a convenient, quick-cooking form.

Grapeseed oil or other oil

1 (12.5-ounce) package brown rice mochi, cut into 1 x 2-inch rectangles (about 2 cups)

Warm a medium cast iron skillet over low heat. When the pan is warm, decrease the heat to low. Brush the pan lightly with oil and add enough mochi slices to fill the pan, keeping them spaced about an inch apart. Cover the pan and cook for 5 minutes on one side, or until the mochi releases easily from the pan (if it sticks, it's not ready yet). Turn the mochi over, replace the cover, and cook for 3 minutes longer, until the mochi has puffed up and feels soft. Remove from the pan. Cook the remaining mochi in the same manner. Serve warm.

Per serving: calories: 123, protein: 3 g, fat: 1 g, carbohydrate: 26 g, fiber: 1 g, sodium: 1 mg

Mochi Waffles: Lay thinly sliced strips of mochi on a hot waffle iron and cook for 5 minutes, or until the mochi has melted and puffed. Serve with warm maple syrup or Lemony Brown Rice Syrup (see below).

Mochi Serving Ideas

Cabbage Rolls: Tuck warm mochi and a teaspoon of sauerkraut inside a cabbage leaf that has been steamed until soft. Sprinkle with a few drops of wheat-free tamari.

Japanese Style: Brush warm mochi with a few drops of wheat-free tamari, then stuff it with 1 teaspoon of finely grated daikon and thinly sliced scallions. Wrap the mochi with a long, rectangular piece of nori.

Kid Style: Spread warm mochi with a little almond butter and all-fruit jam.

Lemony Brown Rice Syrup: Drizzle warm mochi with warmed gluten-free brown rice syrup to which a squeeze of lemon juice has been added.

Strawberry Shake `GLUTEN FREE`

MAKES 4 SERVINGS

Creamy and delicious, this shake is rich in beta-carotene, vitamin C, omega-3 fatty acids, and fiber. It's a nourishing breakfast in a glass!

3 cups hulled fresh or frozen strawberries

2 cups amazake (original, almond, or hazelnut)

1 cup cantaloupe chunks

¼ cup ground flaxseeds, hempseeds, or chia seeds

½ teaspoon sweet white miso (optional)

Put all the ingredients in a blender and process until smooth. Guzzle away!

Per serving: calories: 183, protein: 5 g, fat: 4 g, carbohydrate: 30 g, fiber: 5 g, sodium: 15 mg

CHAPTER THREE

Appetizers

LET'S SAY YOU'RE THROWING A PARTY and you want to impress your friends with your new cooking talents. If you hear the phrase, "Hey, what's that stuff that looks like corrugated cardboard?" you'll know you've lost them. Don't become another health-nut statistic! Wow your guests with fancy, fun-to-eat appetizers that are actually appetizing. Just when they assume that you scrapped the health foods for more traditional fare, blast them with the news that, yes, they just ate tofu and they liked it. Read on, true believers.

Basil Summer Rolls `GLUTEN FREE`

MAKES 4 ROLLS

Delight your guests with these beautiful, delicious rolls. They look especially lovely sliced on a diagonal and arranged on a party platter.

Peanut Sauce

⅔ cup unsweetened creamy peanut butter

3½ tablespoons brown rice vinegar

2 tablespoons wheat-free tamari

2 tablespoons gluten-free brown rice syrup

1 teaspoon peeled and minced fresh ginger

1 clove garlic, crushed (1 teaspoon)

⅛ teaspoon crushed red pepper flakes (optional)

¼ cup water

Rolls

8 rice paper rounds (8 inches in diameter)

1 cup sliced ready-made baked marinated tofu

1 cup whole fresh basil or mint leaves

1 cup seeded and sliced cucumber

To make the sauce, combine the peanut butter, vinegar, tamari, syrup, ginger, garlic, and optional red pepper flakes in a small bowl. Gradually add the water, stirring constantly, until the sauce is smooth and creamy. Adjust the seasonings to taste.

To make the rolls, fill a shallow bowl or pan with warm water. Soak 2 rice paper rounds in the warm water for 30 to 60 seconds, until pliable. Remove from the water and put on a plate. Use 2 rice paper rounds for each wrapper, as this will help to prevent them from tearing. Place a few strips of the tofu, a few basil leaves, and a few slices of cucumber in the center of each wrapper. Top with a few teaspoons of the Peanut Sauce. Fold the bottom edge of the wrapper over the filling, and then roll the wrapper tightly around the filling. Fold in the sides midway and then continue rolling. Transfer the roll to a plate and cover with dampened paper towels (to keep the rice paper from drying out). Make 3 more rolls in the same manner. Slice the finished rolls in half on a diagonal. Serve with the remaining Peanut Sauce for dipping.

Note: Basil Summer Rolls can be made 6 hours in advance. Wrap them in dampened paper towels (to keep them from drying out), put them in a storage container, and refrigerate. Slice the rolls just before serving.

Per roll: calories: 444, protein: 24 g, fat: 24 g, carbohydrate: 33 g, fiber: 3 g, sodium: 847 mg

Easy Scallion Hummus `GLUTEN FREE`

This popular dip is super easy and inexpensive to make. The addition of scallions adds a special touch you're sure to enjoy. Serve it with crudités or brown rice crackers.

1 can (15 ounces) chickpeas, drained and rinsed

3 scallions, chopped

Juice of 1 lemon

2 tablespoons tahini

½ teaspoon sea salt

Put all the ingredients in a blender or food processor and process until smooth. Add just enough water to facilitate processing and achieve the desired consistency. Stored in a sealed container in the refrigerator, Easy Scallion Hummus will keep for 5 days.

Per ¼ cup: calories: 96, protein: 5 g, fat: 3 g, carbohydrate: 11 g, fiber: 4 g, sodium: 140 mg

Fruit Pizzas

Kids love to make and eat this sweet version of pizza. It's not only pretty, it's a great way to make eating fruit fun. For variety, use apple, peach, or pear slices for some or all of the fruit, and try blackberries instead of blueberries. Happy pizza making!

4 whole-grain pita rounds

1½ cups unsweetened apple butter

1 kiwi fruit, peeled and sliced into rounds

½ cup sliced fresh strawberries

½ cup fresh raspberries

½ cup fresh blueberries

Ground cinnamon, for dusting

Spread each pita round with a few tablespoons of the apple butter. Top with one with some the fruit, arranged in an attractive pattern. Dust with the cinnamon. Slice the pizzas into wedges and serve.

Warm Fruit Pizzas: Preheat the oven to 350 degrees F. Arrange the whole pizzas on a baking sheet. Warm in the oven for 5 to 10 minutes. Slice and serve.

Per pizza: calories: 391, protein: 8 g, fat: 1 g, carbohydrate: 83 g, fiber: 10 g, sodium: 311 mg

Nori Maki Sushi Bites `GLUTEN FREE`

MAKES 24 PIECES

Don't be intimidated when it comes to making sushi; it's easier than you think once you get the knack of it. All you need is a sushi mat and the right ingredients to be able to dazzle your friends with your sushi-making finesse.

3 cups Pressure-Cooked Brown Rice (page 86)

3 sheets toasted nori

1 cup sliced ready-made baked marinated tofu, cut into long, thin strips

1 cup sliced avocado, cut into long, thin strips

1 cup sliced cucumber, cut into long, thin strips

½ cup drained pickled ginger

Wheat-free tamari, for dipping

Fill a small bowl with water (to use for your hands) and keep a damp cloth nearby. Set out all the ingredients in a row. You will also need a plate and a serving platter for the finished sushi bites.

Place a sushi mat on a dry, flat work surface, with the bamboo running horizontally. Place 1 sheet of nori on top of the mat, shiny-side down and the perforated lines in the nori running vertically.

Dip your hands in the water to prevent the rice from sticking to them. Scoop about 1 cup of rice with your hands and spread it evenly over the nori. Smooth out the rice, keeping a 1½-inch margin of nori uncovered at the top and covering the remaining portion of the nori right up to the edges.

Place a few strips of the tofu, avocado, and cucumber close together in a horizontal line in the center of the rice. Top with some of the pickled ginger. Place your thumbs under the mat, lifting the nori up and over the filling. Tightly roll the rice and nori over the filling, snugly tucking the filling inside. Give the roll a gentle squeeze, and then pull the top part of the mat out so it isn't rolled into the sushi (that would be just a little too much fiber!). Continue rolling the sushi to the end of the nori sheet. When it is completely rolled, use the mat to squeeze the roll tightly, which will make it more secure. Release the mat and place the finished sushi roll on a plate. Repeat this process with the remaining nori, rice, and filling ingredients.

When all the rolls have been made, lightly moisten the blade of a sharp knife and slice each roll in half crosswise, wiping the blade and remoistening it as needed for clean cuts. Slice the 2 pieces in half crosswise, and then slice all 4 pieces in half crosswise to create 8 pieces. Arrange the pieces in a decorative pattern on a party platter and get ready for your guests to ooh and aah.

Per 4 pieces: calories: 257, protein: 10 g, fat: 10 g, carbohydrate: 27 g, fiber: 7 g, sodium: 635 mg

Mushroom-Leek Phyllo Purses

MAKES 6 PURSES

These popular appetizers are crispy on the outside and filled with tender, juicy mushrooms and leeks on the inside. There's nothing better!

Filling

1 teaspoon grapeseed oil or other oil

1 tablespoon water

4 cups button mushrooms, cleaned and thinly sliced

1 teaspoon dried basil

½ teaspoon dried sage

Sea salt

4 cups sliced leeks (see note)

2 teaspoons mirin

2 teaspoons sweet white miso, mixed with ¼ cup cold water

Ground black pepper

To make the filling, heat the oil and 1 teaspoon of the water in a large skillet over medium-high heat. Add the mushrooms, basil, sage, and a sprinkle of salt. Cover and steam for 5 minutes, or until the mushrooms are tender. Add the leeks, mirin, and a few more pinches of salt. Cook and stir for 10 minutes, uncovered. Add the diluted miso and pepper to taste. Simmer for 5 minutes longer, until the liquid evaporates. Transfer to a bowl to cool.

Preheat the oven to 350 degrees F. Lightly oil a baking sheet.

To make the phyllo purses, place 2 sheets of the phyllo dough on a dry, flat work surface. Using a pastry brush, brush the top sheet of phyllo dough with oil. Place 2 more sheets of phyllo dough on top of the other sheets, and brush the top sheet of phyllo dough with oil. Repeat this process 1 more time, using a total of 6 sheets of phyllo dough. Cut the layered phyllo dough into 6 small squares.

Purse

**6 sheets phyllo dough,
thawed**

**1 cup grapeseed oil
or other oil, for brushing**

In the center of each square, place about ⅓ cup of the mushroom mixture. Bring all 4 corners of the phyllo dough up to meet in the center over the filling and squeeze and twist the ends together to create a purse. Repeat with the remaining squares.

Place the finished purses on the prepared baking sheet and lightly brush them with a little more oil. Bake for 30 minutes, or until golden.

Note: To clean leeks, fill a large bowl with cold water and soak the leeks in it for 5 minutes. Rinse each leek with cold running water. Slice the leeks in half lengthwise. Rinse them again, making sure to wash off all the dirt hiding inside the leaves.

Per purse: calories: 456, protein: 5 g, fat: 39 g, carbohydrate: 23 g, fiber: 3 g, sodium: 151 mg

Blueberry Salsa GLUTEN FREE

MAKES 2 CUPS

This unexpected combination of ingredients makes for a fun appetizer at parties. Your guests will be surprised to see blueberries in this unique salsa. Serve it with tortilla chips.

2 cups fresh blueberries, coarsely chopped

½ cup diced red or green bell pepper

⅓ cup freshly squeezed lime juice

2 teaspoons minced fresh cilantro

1 teaspoon diced red onion

1 teaspoon minced jalapeño chile

½ teaspoon sea salt

Combine all the ingredients in a medium bowl. Refrigerate for 1 to 3 hours before serving. Stored in a sealed container in the refrigerator, Blueberry Salsa will keep for 5 days.

Per ½ cup: calories: 25, protein: 0 g, fat: 0 g, carbohydrate: 6 g, fiber: 1 g, sodium: 134 mg

Hiyayakko GLUTEN FREE

MAKES 4 SERVINGS

This refreshing Japanese dish is a simple way to serve tofu in the summer.

14 ounces firm tofu, drained

1 teaspoon peeled and finely grated fresh ginger

4 teaspoons thinly sliced scallion

2 teaspoons wheat-free tamari

Cut the tofu into 4 squares and put the pieces on individual serving plates. Top each square with a little of the ginger and scallion and a few drops of the tamari. Serve chilled.

Per serving: calories: 123, protein: 13 g, fat: 6 g, carbohydrate: 3 g, fiber: 1 g, sodium: 162 mg

soups & stews

Nourishing Soups and Stews

Checking the menu, a restaurant customer ordered a bowl of vegetable soup. After a couple of spoonfuls, he saw a circle of wetness right under the bowl on the tablecloth. He called the waitress over and said, "It's all wet down here. The bowl must be cracked."

The waitress said, "You ordered the vegetable soup, didn't you?"

"Yes," he replied.

"Well, maybe it has a leek in it."

—**Milton Berle**

NOTHING IS COZIER THAN HOLDING A STEAMING BOWL OF SOUP in your hands on a cold winter evening. I've always loved the ritual of eating soup—feeling soft cubes of vegetables in my mouth between sips of warm broth. Soup—made with grains, beans, vegetables, or pasta—is part of every cuisine worldwide, and making soup is an enjoyable, earthy experience. If you haven't tried preparing soup from scratch yet, you'll fall in love with the process.

Vegetable Broth GLUTEN FREE

MAKES 8 CUPS

A tasty broth adds flavor and nutrition to soups and stews. It can also be used to enhance sauces and salad dressings.

10 cups water

2 cups sliced carrots

1 cup shredded cabbage

1 cup thinly sliced celery

1 medium onion, sliced

1 cup parsley sprigs

3 dried shiitake mushrooms

3 bay leaves

1 (3-inch) piece kombu

3 cloves garlic, sliced

Put all the ingredients in a large soup pot. Cover and bring to a boil over medium-high heat. Decrease the heat to medium-low and simmer for 1 hour. Strain and discard the solids. Stored in a sealed container, Vegetable Broth will keep for 4 days in the refrigerator or 3 months in the freezer.

Note: Other vegetables may be substituted. You can also use vegetable scraps, such as corn cobs, vegetable peelings, ends of vegetables, or the outer leaves of cabbage or lettuce.

Per cup: calories: 53, protein: 3 g, fat: 1 g, carbohydrate: 7 g, fiber: 4 g, sodium: 87 mg

Ginger-Squash Soup GLUTEN FREE

Nothing is quite as warming as a bowl of soup with ginger and squash. Ginger boosts circulation and aids digestion too.

4 cups vegetable broth or coconut milk

3 cups peeled and cubed butternut squash or other winter squash

1 cup diced onion

½ teaspoon sea salt

⅓ cup finely grated ginger, squeezed (reserve the juice and discard the pulp)

⅓ cup thinly sliced scallions, for garnish

Put the broth, squash, onion, and a pinch of the salt in a medium soup pot. Cover and bring to a boil over medium-high heat. Decrease the heat to low and simmer for 25 minutes, or until the squash is soft.

Using a slotted spoon, transfer the vegetables to a blender or food processor and process until smooth. Return the blended vegetables to the soup pot. Add the remaining salt, ginger juice, and a little water, if needed, to achieve the desired consistency. Simmer for 5 minutes longer. Serve hot, garnished with the scallions.

Per serving: calories: 138, protein: 5 g, fat: 1 g, carbohydrate: 23 g, fiber: 10 g, sodium: 363 mg

Sweet Rice Soup `GLUTEN FREE`

MAKES 4 SERVINGS

Sweet rice is stickier and sweeter than its cousin, regular short-grain brown rice. Complemented by veggies like carrots, corn, and parsnips, this soup is ultra satisfying.

5 cups vegetable broth

½ cup sweet brown rice, rinsed

Pinch sea salt

1 cup cubed carrot

1 cup diced onion

1 cup peeled and cubed parsnip

1½ cups cooked or canned kidney beans, drained and rinsed

1 cup fresh or frozen corn kernels

2 tablespoons sweet white miso, mixed with ¼ cup warm water

¼ cup chopped fresh parsley, for garnish

Combine the broth, rice, and salt in a large soup pot and bring to a boil over medium-high heat. Decrease the heat to low, cover, and simmer for 50 minutes.

Add the carrot, onion, and parsnip and bring to a boil over medium-high heat. Decrease the heat to low and simmer uncovered for 20 minutes, or until the vegetables are soft.

Add the beans, corn, and diluted miso. Simmer for 10 minutes longer. Serve hot, garnished with the parsley.

Note: For maximum digestibility, soak the rinsed rice in water to cover for 6 to 8 hours before cooking. Drain the soaked rice and discard the soaking water.

Per serving: calories: 310, protein: 14 g, fat: 2 g, carbohydrate: 50 g, fiber: 15 g, sodium: 350 mg

Corny Chowder GLUTEN FREE

This creamy soup tastes like sunshine in a bowl. Its gorgeous golden color is sure to bring a smile to your face.

1 tablespoon water

1 teaspoon grapeseed oil or other oil

1 cup diced onion

½ cup diced carrot

½ cup diced celery

½ cup yellow corn grits (polenta)

5 cups vegetable broth

2 cups fresh or frozen corn kernels

2 teaspoons umeboshi vinegar

½ teaspoon sea salt

½ cup toasted pumpkin seeds, for garnish

¼ cup chopped fresh cilantro or parsley, for garnish

Heat the water and oil in a medium soup pot over medium heat. Add the onion and cook and stir for 5 minutes, or until translucent. Add the carrot and celery and cook and stir for 5 minutes. Add the corn grits and cook and stir for 5 minutes, or until they are lightly toasted and aromatic. Stir in the broth, whisking constantly to prevent lumping. Stir in the corn and bring to a boil over medium-high heat. Decrease the heat to low, cover, and simmer for 20 minutes, stirring occasionally. If the soup seems too thick, stir in a little more broth to achieve the desired consistency. Stir in the vinegar and salt. Serve hot, garnished with pumpkin seeds and cilantro.

Per serving: calories: 367, protein: 18 g, fat: 16 g, carbohydrate: 35 g, fiber: 12 g, sodium: 410 mg

Luscious Lentil Soup GLUTEN FREE

MAKES 6 SERVINGS

There are so many reasons to love lentils: they are inexpensive, delicious, high in protein, low in fat, and quick-cooking. When you're in a time crunch or forget to soak beans, lentils are a fast alternative—no soaking required!

1 tablespoon water

1 teaspoon grapeseed oil or other oil

1 cup diced onion

2 cloves garlic, minced (2 teaspoons)

½ teaspoon dried basil

½ teaspoon dried oregano

½ teaspoon dried thyme

½ teaspoon sea salt

1 cup peeled and diced sweet potato

1 cup diced carrot

½ cup diced green cabbage

4 cups vegetable broth

Heat the water and oil in a medium soup pot over medium heat. Add the onion, garlic, basil, oregano, thyme, and a pinch of the salt. Cook and stir for 5 minutes, or until the onion is translucent. Add the sweet potato, carrot, cabbage, and a splash of water, if needed, to prevent the vegetables from sticking to the pot. Cook and stir for 5 minutes longer.

Add the broth, lentils, bay leaves, and kombu and bring to a boil over medium-high heat. Decrease the heat to low, cover, and simmer for 30 minutes, or until the lentils are very soft. For a thinner consistency, add a little more broth. For a thicker consistency, transfer 2 cups of the soup to a blender, process until smooth, and stir back into the pot. Alternately, use an immersion blender directly in the pot to briefly process the soup.

2 cups dried green
or brown lentils, rinsed

2 bay leaves

1 (2-inch) piece kombu,
soaked in water for 10
minutes, drained, and
chopped

1 cup fresh basil leaves,
coarsely chopped

2 teaspoons wheat-free tamari

2 teaspoons umeboshi vinegar

¼ cup minced fresh parsley,
for garnish

Stir in the basil, tamari, vinegar, and remaining salt and simmer for 15 minutes. Serve hot, garnished with the parsley.

Per serving: calories: 164, protein: 9 g, fat: 2 g, carbohydrate: 21 g, fiber: 10 g, sodium: 380 mg

Black Bean Soup `GLUTEN FREE`

MAKES 6 SERVINGS

Who doesn't love earthy black bean soup? Seasoned with cumin and the mild heat of jalapeño chile, this flavorful soup will delight even the pickiest eaters.

1 (2-inch) piece kombu, rinsed, soaked in water for 10 minutes and drained

2 cups dried black beans, soaked for 6 to 12 hours in water to cover

4 cups water, as needed

1 teaspoon grapeseed oil or other oil

1 cup diced onion

½ cup diced red bell pepper

2 tablespoons minced jalapeño chile

1 clove garlic, minced (1 teaspoon)

1 teaspoon sea salt

Put the kombu in a medium saucepan. Drain the beans and put them in the saucepan on top of the kombu. Add enough of the water to cover the beans by 1 inch. Bring to a boil over medium-high heat, skimming off any foam that accumulates at the surface. Boil for 10 minutes, continuing to remove any foam. Decrease the heat to low, cover, and simmer for 1 hour, or until the beans are soft. Occasionally add a small amount of cold water, as needed, to keep the beans covered while they are cooking.

Warm the oil with 2 tablespoons of water in a medium soup pot over medium heat. Add the onion, bell pepper, chile, garlic, and a pinch of the salt and cook and stir for 5 minutes. Add the carrot, celery, cumin, chili powder, and another pinch of the salt and cook and stir for 5 minutes.

1 cup diced carrot

1 cup diced celery

1 teaspoon ground cumin

½ teaspoon chili powder

4 cups vegetable broth

2 cups seeded and diced
fresh tomatoes

¼ teaspoon cayenne (optional)

Ground black pepper

Tofu sour cream, for garnish

Minced fresh chives or
scallions, for garnish

Add the beans, broth, tomatoes, remaining salt, optional cayenne, and pepper to taste. If needed, add a little more broth to achieve the desired consistency. Bring to a boil over medium-high heat. Decrease the heat to low, cover, and simmer for 20 minutes. If a thicker soup is desired, blend half the soup with an immersion blender until smooth. Serve hot, garnished with a dollop of tofu sour cream and a sprinkling of chives.

Per serving: calories: 303, protein: 17 g, fat: 2 g, carbohydrate: 41g, fiber: 15g, sodium: 475 mg

Split Pea Soup `GLUTEN FREE`

MAKES 6 SERVINGS

Split peas cook up thick and creamy in this classic, satisfying soup. It will stick to your ribs when it's cold outside. Try it topped with some crunchy toasted pumpkin seeds or oyster crackers.

1 (2-inch) piece kombu, soaked in water for 10 minutes and drained

2 bay leaves

2 cups dried green split peas, rinsed and drained (see note)

2 tablespoons water

1 teaspoon sesame oil

1 cup diced onion

2 cloves garlic, minced (2 teaspoons)

Put the kombu and bay leaves on the bottom of a large soup pot and put the split peas on top. Cover with water. Bring to a boil over medium-high heat, skimming off any foam that accumulates at the surface. Boil for 10 minutes, continuing to remove any foam. Add a little more water, if needed, to keep the split peas covered. Decrease the heat to low, cover, and simmer for 1 hour, or until the split peas are very soft.

Heat the 2 tablespoons water and oil in a medium skillet over medium heat. Add the onion and garlic and cook and stir for 5 minutes, or until the onion is soft and translucent. Add the celery, carrot, basil, and a pinch of the salt. Cook and stir for 5 minutes, or until all the vegetables are tender. Add a little more water, if needed, to keep the vegetables from sticking to the skillet.

2 stalks celery, diced

½ cup diced carrot

½ teaspoon dried basil

½ teaspoon sea salt

1 tablespoon umeboshi vinegar

Ground black pepper

¼ cup minced fresh parsley,
   for garnish

Add the vegetables, remaining salt, vinegar, and pepper to taste to the split peas. Simmer for 10 minutes. Add a little more water, if needed, to achieve the desired consistency. Stir frequently to prevent scorching. (If the soup burns on the bottom of the pot, carefully pour the soup into a clean pot without scraping the burned portion.) Adjust the seasonings to taste. Serve hot, garnished with the parsley.

Note: For faster cooking and easier digestion, soak the split peas in water to cover for 6 to 8 hours before cooking. Drain and proceed with the recipe as directed.

Per serving: calories: 106, protein: 6 g, fat: 1 g, carbohydrate: 12 g, fiber: 7 g, sodium: 216 mg

Navy Bean Soup GLUTEN FREE

See photo facing page 49

MAKES 4 SERVINGS

Navy beans, like all dried beans, are a high-fiber source of protein. You can make this soup thinner, with more broth, or creamy and thick, depending on the whims of your taste buds.

1 tablespoon water

1 teaspoon grapeseed oil or other oil

1 cup diced carrot

1 cup diced celery

1 cup diced onion

2 cloves garlic, minced (2 teaspoons)

1 teaspoon dried oregano

4 cups vegetable broth

2 cups cooked or canned navy beans, drained and rinsed

1 bay leaf

2 cups chopped kale

1 tablespoon sweet white miso, mixed with ¼ cup water

½ teaspoon sea salt

Ground black pepper

Heat the water and oil in a medium soup pot over medium heat. Add the carrot, celery, onion, garlic, and oregano. Cook and stir for 5 minutes. Add the broth, beans, and bay leaf and bring to a boil over medium-high heat. Decrease the heat to low, cover, and simmer for 30 minutes, or until the vegetables are tender. If you prefer a thicker soup, process half the soup in batches in a blender until smooth and return the blended mixture to the pot.

Add the kale, diluted miso, salt, and pepper to taste. If the soup is too thick, add a little more broth or water to achieve the desired consistency. Cover and simmer for 10 minutes. Serve hot.

Per serving: calories: 256, protein: 13 g, fat: 3 g, carbohydrate: 32 g, fiber: 17 g, sodium: 523 mg

Creamy Cauliflower-Broccoli Soup `GLUTEN FREE`

MAKES 4 SERVINGS

S triking colors and interesting textures contrast beautifully in this thick, white, creamy soup, dotted with buoyant green broccoli and flecks of red bell pepper.

2 tablespoons water

1 cup diced onion

½ cup chopped celery

1 teaspoon minced fresh thyme

Pinch sea salt

4 cups cauliflower florets

2 cups plain almond milk or other nondairy milk

2 cups vegetable broth

2 tablespoons sweet white miso, mixed with 3 tablespoons warm water

1½ cups broccoli florets, steamed

¼ teaspoon ground nutmeg

Ground black pepper

⅓ cup very finely diced red bell pepper, for garnish

Heat the water in a medium soup pot over medium heat. Add the onion, celery, thyme, and salt. Cook and stir for 5 minutes, adding a little more water, if needed. Add the cauliflower, almond milk, and broth and bring to boil over medium-high heat. Decrease the heat to medium-low, cover, and simmer for 25 minutes, or until the vegetables are tender. Stir in the diluted miso.

Process the soup until smooth in small batches in a blender and return the soup to the pot. Alternatively, use an immersion blender directly in the pot.

Add the broccoli, nutmeg, and black pepper to taste. Serve hot, garnished with the red bell pepper.

Per serving: calories: 127, protein: 6 g, fat: 2 g, carbohydrate: 17 g, fiber: 7 g, sodium: 375 mg

Coconut-Curry-Carrot Soup GLUTEN FREE

MAKES 6 SERVINGS

This creamy soup is sweet, nourishing, and satisfying. The turmeric in curry powder is a natural antiseptic and also reduces inflammation.

1 tablespoon water

1 medium onion, diced

1 teaspoon curry powder

1 teaspoon sea salt

6 cups sliced carrots

6 cups vegetable broth

1 can (15 ounces) coconut milk

½ cup chopped fresh cilantro, for garnish

Heat the water in a medium soup pot over medium heat. Add the onion, curry powder, and a pinch of the salt. Cook and stir for 5 minutes. Add a little more water, if needed, to keep the onion from sticking. Add the carrots and cook and stir for 5 minutes. Add the broth and coconut milk and bring to a boil over medium-high heat. Decrease the heat to low, cover, and simmer for 25 minutes, or until the carrots are tender. Stir in the remaining salt and simmer for 5 minutes longer.

Process the soup until smooth in small batches in a blender and return the soup to the pot. Alternatively, use an immersion blender directly in the pot. Add a little more broth, if necessary, to achieve the desired consistency. Serve hot, garnished with the cilantro.

Per cup: calories: 241, protein: 5 g, fat: 17 g, carbohydrate: 14 g, fiber: 8 g, sodium: 503 mg

Noodles in Mushroom Broth `GLUTEN FREE`

This is the fastest meal in the west . . . or east! I like to serve it cool in the summer, with a garnish of sliced lemon. Feel free to use any type of noodles or pasta you like, such as brown rice penne or corn elbow macaroni.

3 dried shiitake mushrooms, soaked in water for 30 minutes, or until soft

4 cups water

1 (2-inch) piece kombu, soaked in water for 10 minutes, drained, and thinly sliced

½ cup carrot matchsticks

½ cup daikon matchsticks

2 tablespoons wheat-free tamari

1 (2-inch) piece fresh ginger, grated and squeezed (reserve the juice, about 1 teaspoon, and discard the pulp)

4 cups cooked whole-grain or gluten-free noodles

2 tablespoons thinly sliced scallion, for garnish

2 teaspoons toasted black or tan sesame seeds, for garnish

Drain the mushrooms and reserve their soaking liquid. Remove and discard the mushroom stems and thinly slice the caps.

Put the water, mushrooms and their soaking liquid, and kombu in a medium saucepan. Bring to a boil over medium-high heat. Add the carrot and daikon. Decrease the heat to low, cover, and simmer for 5 minutes. Add the tamari and ginger juice. Simmer for 5 minutes longer.

Divide the noodles among 4 soup bowls. Pour the hot broth and vegetables over the noodles. Serve at once, garnished with the scallion and sesame seeds.

Note: For variety, cut the carrot and/or daikon into flower shapes instead of matchsticks.

Per serving: calories: 342, protein: 14 g, fat: 4 g, carbohydrate: 63 g, fiber: 6 g, sodium: 619 mg

French Onion Soup

In lieu of cheese, this classic soup is topped with a product called mochi, which is made from brown rice; it can be found in the refrigerated section of your local natural-food store.

2 tablespoons water

1 teaspoon sesame oil

3 cups thinly sliced onions, cut into half-moons

Pinch sea salt

8 dried shiitake mushrooms, soaked in cold water for 30 minutes, or until soft

4 cups vegetable broth

1 (2-inch) piece kombu, soaked in water for 10 minutes and drained

1½ tablespoons wheat-free tamari

2 cups whole-grain croutons

2 cups grated mochi

⅓ cup minced fresh parsley, for garnish

Heat the water and oil in a medium soup pot over medium heat. Add the onions and salt. Cook and stir for 5 minutes, or until the onions are soft and translucent.

Preheat the oven to 350 degrees F.

Drain the mushrooms and reserve their soaking water. Remove and discard the mushroom stems and thinly slice the caps. Add the mushrooms and their soaking water, broth, and kombu to the soup pot. Bring to a boil over medium-high heat. Decrease the heat to low, cover, and simmer for 20 minutes. Remove and discard the kombu. Add the tamari. Simmer for 5 minutes longer.

Ladle the soup into 4 ovenproof soup bowls. Place ½ cup of the croutons on top of each serving and sprinkle with ½ cup of the mochi. Bake for 5 minutes, or until the mochi melts over the soup. Serve hot, garnished with the parsley.

Per serving: calories: 296, protein: 10 g, fat: 4 g, carbohydrate: 52 g, fiber: 9 g, sodium: 569 mg

Arugula with Pecans and Pears, page 59

Navy Bean Soup, page 44

Magical Miso Soup GLUTEN FREE

Miso is a source of beneficial bacteria, which aid digestion. When miso is used in soup, it is soothing and delicious. If you serve miso soup often, try different combinations of vegetables for variety.

4 dried shiitake mushrooms, soaked in 1 ½ cups water for 30 minutes, or until soft

3½ cups water

½ cup diced daikon

½ cup peeled and diced winter squash

1 (2-inch) piece wakame, rinsed, soaked in water for 10 minutes, drained, and finely chopped

2 teaspoons brown rice miso

1 cup thinly sliced daikon greens

1 tablespoon thinly sliced scallion, for garnish

Drain the mushrooms and save the soaking liquid. Remove and discard the mushroom stems and thinly slice the caps. Put the mushroom soaking liquid and the water in a medium saucepan and bring to a boil over medium-high heat. Add the mushrooms, daikon, squash, and wakame. Cover and simmer on low for 5 minutes.

Put the miso in a small bowl. Add a few spoonfuls of the hot soup broth and stir until smooth. Add the diluted miso and daikon greens to the soup. Cover and simmer on low heat for 3 minutes. Serve hot, garnished with the scallion.

Per serving: calories: 38, protein: 2 g, fat: 0 g, carbohydrate: 7 g, fiber: 2 g, sodium: 160 mg

Variations

- Peel and grate a 1-inch piece of fresh ginger and squeeze a few drops of the juice into the soup at the end of cooking.

- Add small cubes of fresh tofu to the soup along with the miso and daikon greens.

- Add ½ cup of cooked beans, grains, or noodles to the soup along with the miso and daikon greens.

Moroccan Vegetable Stew
over Couscous

MAKES 6 SERVINGS

This is a classic Moroccan dish that is usually served over couscous. If you really want to prepare it the traditional Moroccan way, cook it in an earthenware pot called a *tagine*.

2 tablespoons water

1 teaspoon grapeseed oil or other oil

2 medium carrots, very thinly sliced

2 cups peeled and cubed butternut squash

1 cup diced onion

2 cloves garlic, minced (2 teaspoons)

1 teaspoon ground cumin

2 cups cooked or canned chickpeas, drained and rinsed

2 cups thinly sliced seitan

1 can (14 ounces) diced stewed tomatoes

Heat the water and oil in a stewpot over medium heat. Add the carrots, squash, onion, garlic, and cumin. Cook and stir for 5 to 10 minutes, or until the vegetables are tender. Add the chickpeas, seitan, tomatoes, broth, currants, cinnamon, salt, and red pepper flakes and bring to a boil over medium-high heat. Decrease the heat to low, cover, and simmer for 30 minutes.

While the stew is cooking, prepare the couscous according to the package directions.

- 1½ cups vegetable broth
- ⅓ cup currants
- ½ teaspoon ground cinnamon
- ½ teaspoon sea salt
- ⅛ teaspoon crushed red pepper flakes
- 1 cup brown rice couscous
- 2 tablespoons chopped fresh cilantro or parsley, for garnish
- 2 tablespoons lemon zest, for garnish

To serve, ladle the stew over the cooked couscous. Serve hot, garnished with the cilantro and lemon zest.

Note: To add extra flavor to the brown rice couscous, use vegetable broth in place of water for cooking.

Per serving: calories: 620, protein: 56 g, fat: 5 g, carbohydrate: 83 g, fiber: 13 g, sodium: 408 mg

Mom's Vegetarian Beef Stew

Just like Mom used to make but without the beef. Hearty and satisfying, this stew will warm your bones on chilly nights. Thanks, Mom!

2 tablespoons water

1 teaspoon grapeseed oil or other oil

1 cup onion, diced

½ teaspoon sea salt

5 cups peeled and cubed rutabagas

4 large carrots, cut in half lengthwise, and then cut crosswise into 1-inch chunks

2 cups vegetable broth

Ground black pepper

2 cups bite-sized seitan chunks

½ cup frozen green peas

2 tablespoons wheat-free tamari

1 tablespoon kuzu starch, mixed with 2 tablespoons cold water

Heat the water and oil in a large soup pot over medium heat. Add the onion and a pinch of the salt. Cook and stir for 5 minutes, or until the onion is translucent. Add the rutabagas, carrots, broth, remaining salt, and pepper to taste. Bring to a boil over medium-high heat. Decrease the heat to low, cover, and simmer for 25 minutes. Add the seitan, peas, tamari, and kuzu mixture. Cook for 5 minutes longer. Serve hot (with a slice of your favorite bread for dipping, of course).

Per serving: calories: 509, protein: 71 g, fat: 4 g, carbohydrate: 41 g, fiber: 10 g, sodium: 888 mg

CHAPTER FIVE

Ballads for Salads

To remember a successful salad is generally to remember a successful dinner; at all events, the perfect dinner necessarily includes the perfect salad.

— **George Ellwanger**, *Pleasures of the Table*

Salad is the quintessential beginning to any meal. Not only are salads refreshing and visually appealing, they are also nutritious. Including more salads and raw vegetables in your diet will increase your intake of alpha- and beta-carotene, folic acid, lycopene, and vitamins C and E. Please pass the salad!

Green Bean and Beet Salad GLUTEN FREE

MAKES 4 SERVINGS

When a dear friend served this salad to me at her home, I immediately fell in love with it. She graciously shared her recipe, which I now pass on to you. The sweetness of the beets, the crunch of the pecans, and the zippy horseradish dressing make this salad a winner.

Salad

½ cup pecans or walnuts

3 medium beets, washed and sliced into thin wedges

2 cups water

Sea salt

2 cups trimmed and sliced green beans (in 2-inch lengths)

3 cups thinly sliced belgian endive or arugula

⅓ cup paper-thin slices vidalia or other sweet onion

Dressing

3 tablespoons freshly squeezed lemon juice

1 tablespoon horseradish mustard or dijon mustard

¼ cup extra-virgin olive oil

½ teaspoon sea salt

Ground black pepper

To toast the pecans, preheat the oven to 350 degrees F. Spread the pecans evenly on a baking sheet and bake for 7 minutes, or until fragrant. Transfer to a small glass bowl to cool.

To make the salad, put the beets, water, and a pinch of the salt in a medium saucepan. Bring to a boil over medium-high heat and cook for 10 minutes. Put the green beans on top of the beets, cover, and cook for 5 minutes, or until the beets and the green beans are tender. Add a little extra water during cooking, if needed. Drain the vegetables and transfer them to a bowl to cool.

To make the dressing, combine the lemon juice and mustard in a small bowl. Stir in the oil. Season with salt and pepper to taste.

Combine the cooled beets and green beans with the endive, onion, pecans, and dressing. Toss lightly to coat. Serve at room temperature or thoroughly chilled.

Per serving: calories: 312, protein: 5 g, fat: 25 g, carbohydrate: 16 g, fiber: 7 g, sodium: 412 mg

Super Slaw GLUTEN FREE

Loaded with enzymes, this colorful slaw is great for digestion. To make the slicing go faster, use a mandoline or a food processor fitted with the slicing blade.

3 cups very thinly sliced green cabbage

1 cup very thinly sliced red cabbage

1 cup thinly sliced cucumber

½ cup thinly sliced green or red apple

½ cup thinly sliced red radishes

2 tablespoons brown rice vinegar

2 teaspoon umeboshi vinegar

½ teaspoon sea salt

¼ cup sliced almonds

Salad dressing (optional)

Put the green cabbage, red cabbage, cucumber, apple, and radishes in a large glass bowl. Add the brown rice vinegar, umeboshi vinegar, and salt. Use your hands to rub the vinegars and salt into the vegetables and fruit by gently squeezing and pressing. Marinate at room temperature for 30 to 60 minutes, or until the vegetables and fruit are tender and the water is released from them.

Squeeze out the excess water from the vegetables and fruit. Transfer to a serving bowl and top with the almonds. Serve with your favorite dressing, if you wish.

Per serving: calories: 69, protein: 2 g, fat: 3 g, carbohydrate: 6 g, fiber: 3 g, sodium: 811 mg

Corn and Black Bean Salad `GLUTEN FREE`

MAKES 4 SERVINGS

This colorful salad is a delightful combination of flavors and textures. Served over a bed of greens, it makes a complete meal.

2 cups cooked or canned black beans, drained and rinsed

1 cup fresh or frozen corn kernels, cooked and drained

1 cup diced celery

½ cup diced red bell pepper

⅓ cup minced fresh cilantro or parsley

⅓ cup thinly sliced scallions

¼ cup extra-virgin olive oil

2 tablespoons freshly squeezed lime juice

½ teaspoon ground cumin

½ teaspoon chili powder

Sea salt

Ground black pepper

Dash cayenne (optional)

Combine the beans, corn, celery, bell pepper, cilantro, scallions, oil, lime juice, cumin, and chili powder in a large bowl and mix well. Season with salt and pepper to taste. Add a dash of cayenne, if desired. Mix again. Cover tightly and refrigerate for 1 to 3 hours before serving. Serve thoroughly chilled.

Per serving: calories: 278, protein: 9 g, fat: 14 g, carbohydrate: 22 g, fiber: 9 g, sodium: 30 mg

Tuscan Spring Salad GLUTEN FREE

Crunchy pecans, sweet fruit, and refreshing greens merge in this irresistible, luscious salad.

Salad

10 cups baby salad greens

½ cup roasted and sliced pecans

⅓ cup sliced dried figs

⅓ cup sliced dried apricots

Dressing

⅓ cup extra-virgin olive oil

¼ cup balsamic vinegar

½ teaspoon sea salt

Ground black pepper

To make the salad, put the greens, pecans, figs, and apricots in a large salad bowl.

To make the dressing, combine the oil, vinegar, salt, and pepper to taste in a small glass bowl. Whisk until well blended.

Pour the dressing over the salad just before serving. Toss until evenly distributed.

Per serving: calories: 352, protein: 4 g, fat: 28 g, carbohydrate: 20 g, fiber: 6 g, sodium: 312 mg

Broccoli and Carrot Salad GLUTEN FREE

A dd a little green to the usual carrot-raisin combo and you get a beautiful, calcium-rich salad.

Salad

**3 cups broccoli florets,
  lightly steamed and cooled**

2 cups shredded carrots

**½ cup toasted pumpkin
  seeds or walnuts**

2 tablespoons currants

Dressing

⅓ cup vegan mayonnaise

2 teaspoons dijon mustard

**2 teaspoons gluten-free
  brown rice syrup**

**2 teaspoons apple cider
  vinegar or brown rice vinegar**

½ teaspoon sea salt

To make the salad, combine the broccoli, carrots, pumpkin seeds, and currants in a large glass bowl.

To make the dressing, combine all the dressing ingredients in a small glass bowl and whisk until well blended.

Pour the dressing over the salad and gently toss until evenly coated. Cover and refrigerate for at least 1 hour before serving.

Per serving: calories: 295, protein: 12 g, fat: 21 g, carbohydrate: 17 g, fiber: 3 g, sodium: 433 mg

Arugula with Pecans and Pears GLUTEN FREE

See photo facing page 48

Arugula's bitter-spicy flavor is perfectly complemented by the sweetness of the pears and the crunch of the pecans in this elegant salad.

Salad

½ **cup pecans**

10 **cups arugula**

1 **cup thinly sliced pear**

Dressing

⅓ **cup extra-virgin olive oil**

¼ **cup balsamic vinegar**

¼ **teaspoon sea salt**

To toast the pecans, preheat the oven to 350 degrees F. Spread the pecans on a baking sheet and bake for 7 minutes. Transfer to a bowl to cool.

To make the salad, put the arugula in a large salad bowl and top with the pear.

To make the dressing, combine the oil, vinegar, and salt in a small bowl and whisk until well blended.

Just before serving, add the dressing and pecans to the arugula and pear and toss until evenly combined.

Per serving: calories: 309, protein: 3 g, fat: 28 g, carbohydrate: 9 g, fiber: 6 g, sodium: 166 mg

Cucumber Salad `GLUTEN FREE`

Try cooling off with this salad on a hot summer day.

Salad

⅓ cup finely diced red onion

1 tablespoon brown rice vinegar

1 teaspoon sea salt

2 medium English cucumbers

Dressing

⅓ cup vegan mayonnaise

¼ cup brown rice vinegar

¼ cup gluten-free brown
  rice syrup

½ teaspoon sea salt

⅓ cup minced fresh dill

To make the salad, put the onion in a small glass bowl. Add the vinegar and a few pinches of the salt. Rub the salt and vinegar into the onion. Let marinate at room temperature while you prepare the rest of the salad.

Peel alternate lengthwise strips of the cucumber skin to create a striped pattern. Thinly slice the cucumbers into rounds and transfer to a large glass bowl. Add the remaining salt and lightly rub it into the cucumbers. Marinate at room temperature for 1 hour. Gently squeeze out the excess water from the cucumbers and transfer them to a clean bowl.

To make the dressing, combine the mayonnaise, vinegar, syrup, and salt in a small bowl and whisk until well blended. Pour the dressing over the cucumbers. Add the dill and gently stir to combine. Cover and refrigerate for 1 hour before serving.

Per serving: calories: 142, protein: 1 g, fat: 8 g, carbohydrate: 15 g, fiber: 1 g, sodium: 866 mg

Goddess Salad `GLUTEN FREE`

MAKES 4 SERVINGS

Combine any of your favorite vegetables in this tasty and colorful salad, loaded with vitamins, minerals, and disease-fighting antioxidants. It will make you look and feel like a goddess!

Salad

10 cups chopped romaine lettuce, green leaf lettuce, and/or baby salad greens

½ cup coarsely grated carrot

1 small cucumber, peeled and sliced into rounds

½ cup finely shredded red cabbage

½ cup alfalfa sprouts

¼ cup sunflower seeds (optional)

Dressing

⅓ cup extra-virgin olive oil

¼ cup balsamic vinegar

1 tablespoon maple syrup

1¼ teaspoons dijon mustard

½ teaspoon sea salt

Dash ground black pepper

To make the salad, combine all the salad ingredients in a large salad bowl.

To make the dressing, combine all the dressing ingredients in a small bowl and whisk until well blended.

Pour the dressing over the salad just before serving. Toss until evenly combined.

Per serving: calories: 250, protein: 3 g, fat 21 g, carbohydrate: 12 g, fiber: 3 g, sodium: 360 mg

Dandy Salad with Warm Dressing

MAKES 4 SERVINGS

Dandelion greens are a detoxifying green vegetable, chock-full of calcium, vitamins A and K, and the antioxidant lutein, which is important for good vision.

Salad

4 tablespoons grapeseed oil

4 strips tempeh bacon

10 cups young dandelion greens, rinsed, patted dry, and chopped into bite-sized pieces

Dressing

1 cup plain almond milk

¼ cup gluten-free brown rice syrup

2 tablespoons apple cider vinegar

1 tablespoon kuzu or arrowroot starch, mixed with 2 tablespoons cold water

½ teaspoon sea salt

To make the salad, heat the oil in a medium cast iron skillet over medium heat. When the oil is hot, add the tempeh bacon. Fry each side for 3 minutes, or until golden. Transfer to a plate to cool. When it is cool to the touch, crumble it with your hands or chop it finely.

Put the dandelion greens in a large salad bowl.

To make the dressing, combine all the dressing ingredients in a small saucepan. Bring to boil over medium-high heat, stirring constantly. Decrease the heat to low and simmer for 1 minute. Remove from the heat and stir in half of the tempeh bacon.

Drizzle the warm dressing over the dandelion greens and toss to evenly coat. Serve at once, garnished with the remaining tempeh bacon.

Note: Select small young dandelion greens, as they will not be as bitter as larger, older ones.

Per serving: calories: 162, protein: 7 g, fat: 10 g, carbohydrate: 25 g, fiber: 7 g, sodium: 569 mg

Mom's Potato Salad GLUTEN FREE

Here's a new take on a beloved classic. This dish is always popular at family picnics.

Salad

5 medium red-skinned potatoes

Pinch sea salt

⅔ cup minced celery

⅓ cup minced onion

⅓ cup minced fresh parsley

Dressing

1½ cups vegan mayonnaise

2 tablespoons apple cider vinegar

1 teaspoon yellow mustard

Sea salt

Ground black pepper

To make the salad, put the potatoes in a medium-large saucepan and cover with cold water. Add the salt and bring to a boil over medium-high heat. Decrease the heat to medium-low, partially cover, and cook for 20 minutes, or until the potatoes are fork-tender and the skins split. Do not overcook. Drain the potatoes and transfer them to a plate to cool. When they are cool enough to handle, peel and dice them and put them in a large bowl.

Add the celery, onion, and parsley to the cooled potatoes.

To make the dressing, combine the mayonnaise, vinegar, and mustard in a small bowl and whisk until well blended. Pour over the potatoes and gently mix until evenly distributed. Season with salt and pepper to taste and gently mix again. Cover and refrigerate for at least 1 hour before serving.

Per serving: calories: 386, protein: 3 g, fat: 27 g, carbohydrate: 35 g, fiber: 3 g, sodium: 228 mg

Mom's Millet Salad: Replace the potatoes with 6 cups of cooked, cooled, and cubed millet.

Mom's Rutabaga Salad: Replace the potatoes with 6 cups of peeled, cubed, and cooked rutabagas.

Israeli Salad GLUTEN FREE

MAKES 4 SERVINGS

Simple and refreshing, this salad nicely complements heavier fare, such as stews and beans.

Salad

⅓ cup diced red onion

3 tablespoons freshly squeezed lemon juice

Several pinches sea salt

10 cups chopped romaine lettuce

2 miniature cucumbers, peeled and diced (about 2 cups)

1 small tomato, seeded and diced

½ cup diced red or green bell pepper

⅓ cup pitted black olives (optional)

¼ cup chopped fresh parsley

Dressing

⅓ cup extra-virgin olive oil

3 tablespoons freshly squeezed lemon juice

Sea salt

Ground black pepper

To make the salad, put the onion in a small glass bowl. Add the lemon juice and salt and rub them into the onion. Let marinate while you prepare the rest of the salad.

Combine the lettuce, cucumbers, tomato, bell pepper, optional olives, and parsley in a large salad bowl.

To make the dressing, combine the oil and lemon juice in a small bowl and whisk until well blended. Season with salt and pepper to taste.

Just before serving, pour the dressing over the salad and toss until evenly distributed.

Per serving: calories: 199, protein: 3 g, fat: 17 g, carbohydrate: 7 g, fiber: 4 g, sodium: 17 mg

Waldorf Salad GLUTEN FREE

Waldorf salad was first served at New York's famed Waldorf Astoria Hotel in 1896. The salad was not the invention of a chef but the maître d'hôtel (dining room manager), Oscar Tschirky. The original salad contained only apples, celery, and mayonnaise. Walnuts were added later and became an integral part of the recipe. I like the addition of cabbage for extra nutrition, flavor, and crunch.

4 red apples (any variety), cored and sliced

1 cup shredded Chinese cabbage

1 cup thinly sliced celery

1 cup vegan mayonnaise

⅓ cup currants

⅓ cup chopped walnuts

Put all the ingredients in a large salad bowl and mix until evenly combined. Cover and refrigerate for 1 hour before serving.

Per serving: calories: 302, protein: 2 g, fat: 22 g, carbohydrate: 24 g, fiber: 4 g, sodium: 158 mg

Clear Noodle Salad

MAKES 4 SERVINGS

Mung bean noodles give this dish exotic appeal. Fresh ginger paired with lime juice and soy sauce make an irresistible combination of Asian flavors.

Salad

8 ounces mung bean noodles (bean threads)

2 cups carrot matchsticks

1 cup shredded green cabbage

2 celery stalks, thinly sliced on a diagonal

2 radishes, cut in half and thinly sliced into half-moons

Dressing

2 tablespoons maple syrup

1½ tablespoons wheat-free tamari

1 tablespoon brown rice vinegar

1 tablespoon freshly squeezed lime juice

1 (1-inch) piece fresh ginger, grated and squeezed (reserve the juice, about ½ teaspoon, and discard the pulp)

Garnishes

4 to 6 lettuce leaves

½ cup crushed peanuts

¼ cup chopped fresh cilantro

2 tablespoons thinly sliced scallion

Crushed red pepper flakes (optional)

To make the salad, put the noodles in a heatproof bowl. Pour boiling water over them and let soak for 15 minutes, or until softened. Drain, rinse under cool water, and cut into 3-inch lengths. Transfer the noodles to a large glass bowl. Add the carrots, cabbage, celery, and radishes.

To make the dressing, put the syrup, tamari, vinegar, lime juice, and ginger juice in a small saucepan. Warm on low heat for 5 minutes.

Pour the dressing over the noodles and vegetables and toss gently to combine.

Arrange the lettuce leaves on 4 individual plates and top with the salad. Garnish with the peanuts, cilantro, scallion, and optional red pepper flakes.

Per serving: calories: 366, protein: 7 g, fat: 9 g, carbohydrate: 61 g, fiber: 5 g, sodium: 396 mg

Tempeh Mock Tuna Salad [GLUTEN FREE]

See photo facing page 96

See photo facing page 96

MAKES 4 SERVINGS

S ail the high seas of your taste buds with this vegan rendition of traditional tuna salad. It's wonderful on its own or stuffed into a pita pocket with shredded lettuce and grated carrot.

½ cup minced red onion

2 tablespoons freshly squeezed lemon juice

Sea salt

8-ounces gluten-free tempeh

⅔ cup water

2 teaspoons dijon mustard

½ teaspoon miso (any variety)

⅔ cup vegan mayonnaise

½ cup pickle relish

1 celery stalk, minced

1 teaspoon celery seeds

Ground black pepper

Put the onion in a small glass bowl. Add 1 tablespoon of the lemon juice and a few pinches of salt and rub them into the onion. Let marinate while you prepare the rest of the salad.

Steam the tempeh in a steamer basket over boiling water for 15 minutes. Transfer to a plate to cool. When the tempeh is cool enough to handle, coarsely grate or crumble it.

Transfer the tempeh to a medium saucepan and add the water. Combine the mustard, miso, and remaining tablespoon of lemon juice in a small bowl and mix until well blended. Pour over the tempeh and bring to a boil over medium-high heat. Decrease the heat to low, cover, and simmer for 20 minutes. Uncover and simmer for about 3 minutes, or until the liquid evaporates. Transfer the tempeh to a large bowl to cool.

Add the onion, mayonnaise, relish, celery, and celery seeds to the tempeh. Mix well. Season with salt and pepper to taste and mix again. Serve at once or thoroughly chilled.

Per serving: calories: 334, protein: 11 g, fat: 24 g, carbohydrate: 20 g, fiber: 5 g, sodium: 556 mg

Chickpea Mock Tuna Salad: Replace the tempeh with 2 cups cooked or canned chickpeas, drained and rinsed. Marinate the onion as directed. Mash the chickpeas with the remaining tablespoon of lemon juice and the mustard and miso. Stir in the remaining ingredients. Serve at once or thoroughly chilled.

Summer Pasta Salad GLUTEN FREE

MAKES 6 SERVINGS

Your family and friends will know it's officially summer when this cheery dish appears on the scene.

Salad

3 cups button mushrooms, cleaned and quartered

Sea salt

1 cup very thinly sliced yellow summer squash (in half-moons)

1 cup broccoli florets

1 cup cauliflower florets

½ cup frozen green peas

14 ounces whole-grain or gluten-free spiral pasta, cooked according to package directions

1 cup cooked or canned kidney beans, drained and rinsed

½ cup drained and quartered artichoke hearts (packed in oil or water)

⅓ cup sliced black olives

¼ cup minced fresh parsley

¼ cup drained and minced oil-packed sun-dried tomatoes

¼ cup pine nuts

To make the salad, put the mushrooms in a saucepan. Sprinkle them with a few pinches of salt and add 2 tablespoons of water. Cover and cook over medium-high heat for 5 minutes, or until the mushrooms have softened.

Put a few inches of water in a medium saucepan and bring to a boil over medium-high heat. Drop the squash into the boiling water and cook for less than 1 minute, until just crisp-tender. Remove the squash with a slotted spoon and transfer to a colander. Rinse under cold water. Repeat this process with the broccoli, cauliflower, and peas.

Combine the vegetables, pasta, beans, artichoke hearts, olives, parsley, sun-dried tomatoes, and pine nuts in a large bowl.

Dressing

¼ cup extra-virgin olive oil

¼ cup freshly squeezed orange juice

3 tablespoons red wine vinegar or brown rice vinegar

1 teaspoon dried Italian seasoning

Sea salt

Ground black pepper

To make the dressing, combine the oil, orange juice, vinegar, and herbs in a small bowl and whisk until well blended. Season with salt and pepper to taste.

Drizzle the dressing over the salad and toss gently. Cover and refrigerate for at least 1 hour before serving.

Per serving: calories: 319, protein: 12 g, fat: 16 g, carbohydrate: 30 g, fiber: 8 g, sodium: 163 mg

Orange-Cucumber Salad with Wakame [GLUTEN FREE]

MAKES 6 SERVINGS

Sweet, tart, crunchy, and refreshing—this dish has it all.

4 cups peeled and very thinly sliced English cucumber

1 tablespoon umeboshi vinegar

½ teaspoon sea salt

1 (6-inch) strip dried wakame, rinsed

½ cup freshly squeezed orange juice

2 oranges, peeled and sliced into half-moons or segmented

1 tablespoon brown rice vinegar

1 tablespoon maple syrup

2 teaspoons black sesame seeds, preferably toasted

Put the cucumber in a bowl and sprinkle with the umeboshi vinegar and salt. Rub the vinegar and salt into the cucumber and marinate at room temperature for 1 hour.

While the cucumber is marinating, soak the wakame in the orange juice for 10 minutes. Drain the wakame and chop it finely.

After 1 hour, drain the cucumbers and squeeze out the excess liquid. Transfer the cucumbers to a large glass bowl. Add the wakame, oranges, brown rice vinegar, syrup, and sesame seeds. Toss gently. Cover and refrigerate until thoroughly chilled, about 3 hours, before serving.

Per serving: calories: 57, protein: 1 g, fat: 1 g, carbohydrate: 10 g, fiber: 2 g, sodium: 748 mg

CHAPTER SIX

Spectacular Salad Dressings and Sauces

NOTHING DRESSES UP MEALS BETTER THAN FABULOUS SALAD DRESSINGS AND SAUCES. You can easily make them using pure, natural ingredients that contribute nutrition, moisture, flavor, and color to a dish. Fresh herbs, such as scallions and parsley, can be combined with crushed seeds or nuts, cooked vegetables, or puréed beans or grains to create interesting textures and flavor combinations. Add the right ingredients and seasonings, and you'll have an outrageously impressive dressing or sauce. Below are a few ideas for you to experiment with. Let your creativity and personal preferences guide you.

For bitterness add:
- fresh herbs (such as cilantro, mint, or parsley)
- sesame seeds
- steamed and blended dark leafy greens (such as arugula or kale)
- toasted, crushed walnuts

For pungency add:
- fresh ginger
- garlic
- raw onion
- scallions
- shallots

For richness add:
- cooked and puréed starchy vegetables (such as carrots, parsnips, or winter squash)
- crushed, roasted seeds, or nuts
- grapeseed oil, extra-virgin olive oil, or sesame oil
- mashed avocado
- nut or seed butter
- tofu

For saltiness add:
- miso
- wheat-free tamari
- sea salt
- sea vegetable powder
- umeboshi plum paste

For sourness add:
- apple cider, balsamic, or brown rice vinegar
- freshly squeezed lemon, lime, or orange juice

For sweetness add:
- apple juice
- barley malt, brown rice, or maple syrup
- cooked and puréed sweet vegetables (such as carrots, onions, or winter squash)
- thinned all-fruit jam

Mom's Dynamite Greens Dressing `GLUTEN FREE`

MAKES ABOUT 1½ CUPS

I can always count on finding this in Mom's fridge. She swears I gave her the original recipe, but I know she was the mastermind behind tweaking it to its current formula. It's reminiscent of a honey-mustard dressing, sweet as Mom. Serve it over steamed veggies, a salad, or anything you like.

½ cup maple syrup or gluten-free brown rice syrup

⅓ cup extra-virgin olive oil

¼ cup yellow mustard

¼ cup apple cider vinegar

1½ tablespoons wheat-free tamari

Combine all the ingredients in a dressing bottle. Seal tightly and shake until well combined. Stored in a sealed glass bottle in the refrigerator, Mom's Dynamite Greens Dressing will keep for 3 weeks.

Per 2 tablespoons: calories: 92, protein: 1 g, fat: 6 g, carbohydrate: 9 g, fiber: 0 g, sodium: 176 mg

Balsamic Vinaigrette `GLUTEN FREE`

MAKES ABOUT 1 CUP

This scrumptious dressing is not only great on salads but it also makes a terrific marinade for tofu and tempeh.

⅓ cup extra-virgin olive oil

¼ cup balsamic vinegar

¼ cup gluten-free brown rice syrup or maple syrup

2 tablespoons freshly squeezed orange juice

Sea salt

Ground black pepper

Combine the oil, vinegar, syrup, orange juice, and salt and pepper to taste in a dressing bottle. Seal tightly and shake until well combined. Stored in a sealed glass bottle in the refrigerator, Balsamic Vinaigrette will keep for 5 days.

Per 2 tablespoons: calories: 104, protein: 0 g, fat: 8 g, carbohydrate: 7 g, fiber: 0 g, sodium: 3 mg

Creamy Italian Dressing GLUTEN FREE

MAKES ABOUT 1½ CUPS

This is a low-fat version of the popular dressing found at every salad bar. Now you can enjoy all of the flavor without all the calories!

1 cup soft tofu

1 tablespoon brown rice vinegar or apple cider vinegar

1 tablespoon extra-virgin olive oil

1 teaspoon dried Italian seasoning

½ teaspoon minced garlic

½ teaspoon sea salt

Combine all the ingredients in a blender and process until smooth. Add a little water, if necessary, to achieve the desired consistency. Stored in a sealed glass bottle in the refrigerator, Creamy Italian Dressing will keep for 5 days.

Per 2 tablespoons: calories: 24, protein: 1 g, fat: 2 g, carbohydrate: 1 g, fiber: 0 g, sodium: 91 mg

Creamy Tahini Dressing GLUTEN FREE

MAKES ABOUT 1 CUP

Rich and creamy, this dressing makes simple steamed vegetables taste luscious. Umeboshi plums are highly alkalizing and are great for enhancing digestion.

½ cup water or unsweetened apple juice

¼ cup tahini

¼ cup minced onion, parsley, or scallion

1 umeboshi plum, pitted

Combine all the ingredients in a blender and process until smooth. Stored in a sealed glass bottle in the refrigerator, Creamy Tahini Dressing will keep for 3 days.

Per 2 tablespoons: calories: 45, protein: 1 g, fat: 4 g, carbohydrate: 2 g, fiber: 1 g, sodium: 92 mg

Lemon-Sesame Dressing `GLUTEN FREE`

MAKES ABOUT 1 CUP

The crunch of calcium-rich sesame seeds adds a pleasant contrast of texture and flavor to this light dressing.

¼ cup extra-virgin olive oil

¼ cup unsweetened apple juice

3 tablespoons freshly squeezed lemon juice

2 tablespoons wheat-free tamari

2 tablespoons toasted sesame seeds

Combine all the ingredients in a dressing bottle. Seal tightly and shake until well combined. Stored in a sealed glass bottle in the refrigerator, Lemon-Sesame Dressing will keep for 5 days.

Per 2 tablespoons: calories: 82, protein: 1 g, fat: 8 g, carbohydrate: 2 g, fiber: 0 g, sodium: 231 mg

Miso Vinaigrette `GLUTEN FREE`

MAKES ABOUT 1 CUP

Simple and delicious, this fat-free dressing contain miso, which provides friendly bacteria that aid digestion.

⅓ cup sweet white miso

⅓ cup unsweetened apple juice or water

¼ cup brown rice vinegar

2 tablespoons minced fresh chives

Combine all the ingredients in a small bowl and whisk until well blended. Stored in a sealed glass bottle in the refrigerator, Miso Vinaigrette will keep for 3 days.

Per 2 tablespoons: calories: 28, protein: 1 g, fat: 1 g, carbohydrate: 4 g, fiber: 1 g, sodium: 257 mg

Zippy Citrus Dressing `GLUTEN FREE`

This refreshing dressing will perk up any salad. Feel free to add your favorite fresh herbs in place of or in addition to the cilantro.

- ⅓ cup extra-virgin olive oil
- ⅓ cup freshly squeezed orange juice
- 2 tablespoons freshly squeezed lime juice
- 2 tablespoons minced fresh cilantro
- 2 teaspoons stone ground mustard
- 2 teaspoons gluten-free brown rice syrup or maple syrup
- ½ teaspoon sea salt
- Ground black pepper

Combine all the ingredients in a small bowl, adding pepper to taste. Whisk until well combined. Stored in a sealed glass bottle in the refrigerator, Zippy Citrus Dressing will keep for 3 days.

Per 2 tablespoons: calories: 24, protein: 0 g, fat: 2 g, carbohydrate: 2 g, fiber: 0 g, sodium: 146 mg

Creamy Pumpkin Seed Dressing GLUTEN FREE

MAKES 2 CUPS

Pumpkin seeds are a rich source of amino acids and zinc, and they taste great too.

1 cup toasted pumpkin seeds

⅓ cup minced fresh parsley or scallions

1 umeboshi plum, pitted and mashed

½ cup water

Pulse the pumpkin seeds in a food processor until finely crushed. Add the parsley and umeboshi plum. Pulse again, adding the water in a slow, steady stream to create a thick and creamy dressing.

Per 2 tablespoons: calories: 29, protein: 2 g, fat: 1 g, carbohydrate: 2 g, fiber: 3 g, sodium: 65 mg

Variations: Replace the pumpkin seeds with toasted sunflower or sesame seeds.

Raspberry–Poppy Seed Dressing GLUTEN FREE

MAKES 1 CUP

Poppy seeds add crunch to this sweet and tasty dressing.

½ cup all-fruit raspberry jam

¼ cup extra-virgin olive oil

2 tablespoons apple cider vinegar or brown rice vinegar

2 teaspoons poppy seeds

2 teaspoons dijon mustard

½ teaspoon sea salt

Combine all the ingredients in a small bowl and whisk until well blended. If the dressing is too thick, whisk in a small amount of water to achieve the desired consistency. Stored in a sealed glass bottle in the refrigerator, Raspberry–Poppy Seed Dressing will keep for 3 weeks.

Per 2 tablespoons: calories: 108, protein: 0 g, fat: 7 g, carbohydrate: 11 g, fiber: 0 g, sodium: 166 mg

Green Goddess Dressing GLUTEN FREE

This recipe is a great way to transform leftover rice into a creamy, rich-tasting dressing that's low in fat.

½ cup water

⅓ cup cooked brown rice

¼ cup minced fresh parsley or scallion

1 umeboshi plum, pitted

1 tablespoon tahini

Combine all the ingredients in a blender and process until smooth. Stored in a sealed glass bottle in the refrigerator, Green Goddess Dressing will keep for 3 days.

Per 2 tablespoons: calories: 21, protein: 1 g, fat: 1 g, carbohydrate: 2 g, fiber: 0 g, sodium: 89 mg

Italian Dressing GLUTEN FREE

You'll love this simple, oil-free version of classic Italian dressing.

2/3 cup vegetable broth

2 tablespoons brown rice vinegar or apple cider vinegar

2 teaspoons minced garlic

1 teaspoon kuzu or arrowroot starch, mixed with 1 tablespoon cold water

1 teaspoon dried Italian seasoning

1 teaspoon gluten-free brown rice syrup

1 teaspoon dijon mustard

½ teaspoon sea salt

Ground black pepper

Combine all the ingredients in a small saucepan, adding pepper to taste. Warm over medium heat, stirring constantly, for about 5 minutes, or until the mixture thickens. Adjust the seasonings to taste. Cool completely before using. Stored in a sealed glass bottle in the refrigerator, Italian Dressing will keep for 1 week.

Per 2 tablespoons: calories: 9, protein: 0 g, fat: 0 g, carbohydrate: 1 g, fiber: 0 g, sodium: 157 mg

Tofu Mayonnaise GLUTEN FREE

Enjoy this cholesterol-free, low-cal mayo in lieu of the usual fat-laden kind.

14 ounces firm tofu

¼ cup gluten-free brown rice syrup

2 tablespoons extra-virgin olive oil

1 tablespoon apple cider vinegar

½ teaspoon sea salt

Combine all the ingredients in a food processor or blender and process until smooth. Stored in a covered container in the refrigerator, Tofu Mayonnaise will keep for 1 week.

Per 2 tablespoons: calories: 41, protein: 2 g, fat: 2 g, carbohydrate: 3 g, fiber: 0 g, sodium: 76 mg

Pea Pesto GLUTEN FREE

This pesto has a gorgeous green hue and an incredible flavor that complements any type of pasta. The addition of peas helps reduce the fat while adding extra fiber.

2 cups fresh basil leaves

1 cup fresh or frozen green peas, cooked and drained

⅓ cup pine nuts

1 tablespoon sweet white miso

2 teaspoons minced garlic

Pinch sea salt

¼ cup water

2 tablespoons extra-virgin olive oil

Put the basil, peas, nuts, miso, garlic, and salt in a food processor and begin processing. With the machine running, slowly add the water and oil in a steady stream through the open feed tube in the lid. Process just until the mixture forms a sticky, somewhat chunky paste. Stored in a covered container in the refrigerator, Pea Pesto will keep for 1 week.

Per ¼ cup: calories: 90, protein: 2 g, fat: 7 g, carbohydrate: 3 g, fiber: 2 g, sodium: 57 mg

Carrot-Beet Marinara Sauce GLUTEN FREE

MAKES 10 CUPS

This creative, no-tomato recipe hails from the macrobiotic community, as tomatoes are used minimally in macrobiotic cooking. This sauce has all the flavor of a good Italian marinara; people don't believe me when I tell them I made it without a single tomato!

2 tablespoons water

1 teaspoon extra-virgin olive oil

1 cup diced onion

2 cloves garlic, minced (2 teaspoons)

1 teaspoon dried oregano

½ teaspoon sea salt

8 carrots, chopped

1 cup chopped celery

2 tablespoons diced beet

4 cups vegetable broth or water

Heat the water and oil in a large saucepan over medium heat. Add the onion, garlic, oregano, and a pinch of the salt. Cook and stir for 5 minutes. Add the carrots, celery, and beet. Cook and stir for 10 minutes. Add enough broth to almost cover the vegetables, and bring to a boil. Decrease the heat to low, cover, and simmer for 30 minutes, or until all of the vegetables are soft and can be easily pierced with a fork.

Transfer one-third of the vegetables to a blender or food processor. Add the vinegar, remaining salt, pepper to taste, turmeric, and enough of the vegetable cooking liquid to create a smooth consistency (about 1 cup). Process until smooth. (Take extra care when processing hot foods, as the steam can sometimes force the blender lid to pop off.) Transfer to a large bowl. Process the remaining vegetables the same way in 2 more batches.

2 tablespoons umeboshi vinegar

Ground black pepper

Pinch ground turmeric

1 cup fresh basil leaves, stemmed and chopped

¼ cup kuzu or arrowroot starch, mixed with ⅓ cup cold water

Return the sauce to the saucepan and add the basil and kuzu mixture. Simmer for 5 minutes, or until the sauce has thickened. Serve hot. Stored in a sealed container, Carrot-Beet Marinara Sauce will keep for 3 days in the refrigerator or 2 months in the freezer.

Per cup: calories: 52, protein: 1 g, fat: 1 g, carbohydrate: 9 g, fiber: 2 g, sodium: 789 mg

Onion Gravy GLUTEN FREE

MAKES ABOUT 2½ CUPS

I love this gravy over millet, brown rice, or just about anything!

2 tablespoons water

1 teaspoon sesame oil

2 cups thinly sliced onions (in half-moons)

1 teaspoon dried basil

Pinch sea salt

1 cup vegetable broth

1 tablespoon sweet white miso, mixed with ¼ cup warm water

2 teaspoons kuzu or arrowroot starch, mixed with ¼ cup cold water

Heat the water and oil in a small saucepan over medium heat. Add the onions, basil, and salt. Cook and stir for 5 minutes, or until the onions are translucent. Add the broth and bring to a boil over medium-high heat. Decrease the heat to medium-low and simmer for 20 minutes. Add the diluted miso and kuzu mixture. Simmer, stirring gently, for about 3 minutes, or until the gravy thickens. Serve hot. Stored in a sealed container in the refrigerator, Onion Gravy will keep for 5 days.

Per ¼ cup: calories: 28, protein: 1 g, fat: 1 g, carbohydrate: 4 g, fiber: 1 g, sodium: 51 mg

Mushroom Gravy GLUTEN FREE

This gravy is perfect for ladling over a mound of Millet-Cauliflower Mash (page 94).

2 tablespoons water

1 teaspoon sesame oil

4 cups sliced button or
   baby portobello mushrooms

½ teaspoon dried thyme

¼ teaspoon dried sage

2 pinches sea salt

Ground black pepper

2 cups vegetable broth

⅓ cup red wine (optional)

2 tablespoons wheat-free
   tamari

2 tablespoons kuzu
   or arrowroot starch, mixed
   with ¼ cup cold water

Heat the water and oil in a medium saucepan over medium heat. Add the mushrooms, thyme, sage, salt, and pepper to taste. Cover and cook until the mushrooms are tender, about 5 minutes. Add the broth, optional wine, and tamari and bring to a boil. Decrease the heat to low and simmer for 10 minutes. Add the kuzu mixture and stir until the gravy has thickened. Serve hot. Stored in a sealed container in the refrigerator, Mushroom Gravy will keep for 5 days.

Per ¼ cup: calories: 25, protein: 2 g, fat: 1 g, carbohydrate: 3 g, fiber: 1 g, sodium: 185 mg

Peanut Sauce GLUTEN FREE

MAKES ABOUT 1 CUP

This sauce is perfect for tossing with noodles or serving as a dip with rice paper rolls.

⅔ **cup unsweetened peanut butter (creamy or chunky)**

½ **cup water**

3 **tablespoons brown rice vinegar**

2 **tablespoons wheat-free tamari**

2 **tablespoons gluten-free brown rice syrup**

1 **teaspoon finely grated ginger, squeezed (reserve the juice and discard the pulp)**

1 **clove garlic, minced (1 teaspoon)**

1 **teaspoon crushed red pepper flakes (optional)**

Put the peanut butter in a small bowl and gradually add the water, a little bit at a time, mixing well to combine. Add the remaining ingredients and stir until well blended. If the sauce is too thick, add more water to achieve the desired consistency.

Per 2 tablespoons: calories: 136, protein: 6 g, fat: 9 g, carbohydrate: 8 g, fiber: 2 g, sodium: 184 mg

CHAPTER SEVEN

Radiant Grains

WHOLE GRAINS HAVE SUSTAINED PEOPLE FROM VIRTUALLY EVERY CULTURE around the world for thousands of years. In Asia, rice and millet formed part of the traditional diet. Corn was the principal food of people living in North and South America and in the Caribbean. The Incans also harvested corn, along with a high-protein grain called quinoa. Northern Europeans consumed rye in the form of pumpernickel bread. Wheat was cultivated in China, Ethiopia, India, Ireland, Spain, and Turkey. Barley was consumed by people living in ancient Egypt, Greece, and Tibet. Northern Africa utilized the tiny grain called teff. You get the picture.

Whole grains are high in fiber, which helps with elimination and detoxification. Grains also contain antioxidants, which help protect against cellular damage, B vitamins, magnesium, and vitamin E. Medical evidence shows that a diet rich in whole grains can help reduce the risk of cancer, diabetes, heart disease, obesity, and stroke. The USDA food pyramid recommends daily consumption of whole grains for optimal health. Dig in and reap the rewards!

Pressure-Cooked Brown Rice `GLUTEN FREE`

MAKES 3 CUPS (ABOUT 4 SERVINGS)

This recipe is one of the basics to master. Once you've gotten savvy with a pressure cooker, you'll be hooked on cooking rice in it. A pressure cooker makes brown rice easier to digest, and the chewy texture it produces is addictive. Cooked rice can be used to make fried rice, rice salad, rice pudding . . . the options are endless!

1½ cups water

1 cup short-grain brown rice, rinsed

Pinch sea salt, or 1 piece (½ inch square) kombu

Put all the ingredients in a medium pressure cooker over medium-high heat. Cover and bring up to full pressure. Decrease the heat to low, put a heat diffuser under the pot, and cook for 50 minutes. When the rice is finished cooking, turn off the heat and let the pressure come down naturally. When the pressure is fully released, unlock and remove the lid. Transfer the rice to a medium serving bowl using a spoon.

Note: For maximum digestibility, soak the uncooked rice for 6 to 12 hours prior to cooking it. I also recommend adding a few drops of brown rice vinegar or lemon juice to the soaking water to help reduce the naturally occurring phytic acid found in grains (phytic acid diminishes the availability of essential minerals). Discard the soaking water and cook the rice with fresh water as directed.

Per serving: calories: 170, protein: 5 g, fat: 2 g, carbohydrate: 35 g, fiber: 2 g, sodium: 50 mg

Veggie Fried Rice GLUTEN FREE

A delicious and pretty way to reinvent leftover cooked rice.

1 tablespoon water

1 teaspoon sesame oil

½ cup diced onion

1 teaspoon peeled and
  minced fresh ginger

1 teaspoon minced garlic

2 pinches sea salt

2 cups sliced button
  mushrooms

½ cup diced carrots

4 cups cooked brown rice

1 cup broccoli florets

½ cup fresh or thawed frozen
  corn kernels

2 teaspoons wheat-free tamari

⅓ cup thinly sliced scallions,
  for garnish

Heat the water and oil in a large skillet or wok over medium heat. Add the onion, ginger, garlic, and a pinch of salt. Cook and stir for 5 minutes. Add the mushrooms, carrots, and another pinch of salt. Cook and stir for 5 minutes, or until the mushrooms are tender. Add the rice, broccoli, corn, and tamari. If necessary, add a small splash of water to prevent the vegetables from sticking to the skillet. Cover and cook for 5 minutes longer, or until the vegetables are brightly colored and tender and the rice is hot. Serve hot, garnished with the scallions.

Per serving: calories: 139, protein: 4 g, fat: 2 g, carbohydrate: 25 g, fiber: 3 g, sodium: 119 mg

Zucchini Rice Patties GLUTEN FREE

See photo between pages 96-97

MAKES 12 PATTIES

Light and lemony, these patties are packed with flavor.

Patties

1 cup finely grated zucchini

1 cup coarsely grated zucchini

1 teaspoon sea salt

4 cups cooked short-grain brown rice, lightly mashed

1 cup minced onion

⅔ cup minced fresh parsley

¼ cup arrowroot starch

¼ cup freshly squeezed lemon juice

2 teaspoons celery seeds

1 teaspoon paprika

½ teaspoon ground black pepper

Coating

1 cup yellow cornmeal

¼ cup arrowroot starch

To make the patties, put the zucchini in a medium bowl and rub the salt into it. Transfer to a strainer and set aside to drain for 20 minutes. (Put the strainer in a bowl or in the sink.)

Squeeze out the excess moisture from the zucchini and put it in a clean bowl. Add the remaining patty ingredients and mix well. Using wet hands, form the mixture into 12 small patties.

For the coating, combine the cornmeal and arrowroot starch on a plate. Dip each patty into the coating to completely cover both sides. Put on a plate.

To fry the patties, heat ½ inch of the oil in a cast iron skillet over medium heat. When the oil is hot, fry the patties for 5 minutes on each side, until lightly browned. Line a plate with paper towels (to absorb the excess oil) and transfer the patties to the plate.

Oil for Frying

**1 cup grapeseed oil
or other oil**

Vegan Tartar Sauce

1 cup vegan mayonnaise

**1½ tablespoons
pickle relish**

2 teaspoons minced onion

**2 teaspoons freshly
squeezed lemon juice**

Garnish

Sea salt

12 lemon wedges

To make the tartar sauce, combine all the ingredients in a small bowl and mix well.

To serve, sprinkle the patties lightly with salt. Garnish each patty with a lemon wedge and a dollop of the tartar sauce. Serve hot.

Per serving: calories: 397, protein: 3 g, fat: 28 g, carbohydrate: 31 g, fiber: 3 g, sodium: 276 mg

Mushroom Rice Pilaf GLUTEN FREE

MAKES 6 SERVINGS

In this recipe, simple brown rice is transformed into an enticing medley of textures and colors. This dish stands well on its own, but you can make it even heartier by topping it with baked marinated tofu.

1 tablespoon water

1 teaspoon grapeseed oil or other oil

½ cup diced onion

2 pinches sea salt

2 cups sliced button mushrooms

½ cup diced celery

¼ cup finely diced carrot

4 cups vegetable broth

1¾ cup long-grain brown rice, rinsed

¼ cup wild rice, rinsed

½ cup toasted slivered almonds (see note)

Heat the water and oil in a large skillet. Add the onion and a pinch of salt. Cook and stir for 5 minutes. Add the mushrooms, celery, carrot, another pinch of salt, and a little splash of water, if needed, to keep the vegetables from sticking to the skillet. Cook and stir for 5 minutes, or until the vegetables are tender.

Add the broth, brown rice, and wild rice. Cover and simmer for 1 hour, until the rice is fluffy and soft. Serve hot, topped with the almonds.

Note: To toast the almonds, preheat the oven to 350 degrees F. Spread the almonds in a single layer on a baking sheet. Bake for 5 minutes, or until fragrant and golden. Alternatively, toast the almonds in a dry skillet over medium-low heat, stirring constantly, until golden.

Per serving: calories: 350 protein: 12 g, fat: 9 g, carbohydrate: 54 g, fiber: 8 g, sodium: 113 mg

Forbidden Black Rice `GLUTEN FREE`

Reserved for the courts of ancient Chinese emperors, this special rice was considered an aphrodisiac. High in iron and other minerals, it was also purported to be a blood tonic. When raw, the rice is ebony, but it turns a deep shade of purple when cooked.

2 tablespoons water

1 teaspoon sesame oil

1 medium onion, diced

1 cup diced carrot

1 teaspoon minced garlic

1 teaspoon peeled and minced fresh ginger

1½ cups chopped seitan (optional)

¾ cup mung bean sprouts

½ cup diced red bell pepper

2 teaspoons wheat-free tamari

3 cups cooked forbidden black rice (follow the directions for Pressure-Cooked Brown Rice, page 86)

½ cup sliced scallions, for garnish

½ cup roasted peanuts, for garnish

Heat the water and oil in a large skillet over medium heat. Add the onion, carrot, garlic, and ginger and cook and stir for 5 minutes.

Add the optional seitan, mung bean sprouts, bell pepper, and a few drops of the tamari. Cook and stir for 5 minutes.

Spoon the rice on top of the cooked vegetables in the skillet and sprinkle with the remaining tamari. Cover and cook over medium heat for 5 minutes, or until the rice is warm and the vegetables are tender. Stir before serving. Serve hot, garnished with the scallions and peanuts.

Per serving: calories: 313, protein: 10 g, fat: 12 g, carbohydrate: 39 g, fiber: 6 g, sodium: 315 mg

Golden Raisin Rice GLUTEN FREE

MAKES 6 SERVINGS

Curry powder gives this rice a pleasing touch of spice. Not a curry fan? Feel free to skip it, as the turmeric will make the rice a sunny shade of yellow.

2 tablespoons water

1 teaspoon sesame oil

1 cup diced onion

½ teaspoon sea salt

1 cup diced carrot

1 teaspoon curry powder

2 cups brown basmati rice, rinsed

1 teaspoon dry mustard

¼ teaspoon ground turmeric

2 cups vegetable broth

2 cups freshly squeezed orange juice

1 cup cooked or canned chickpeas, drained and rinsed

½ cup golden raisins

½ cup frozen green peas

1 cup toasted cashews, for garnish

½ cup minced fresh cilantro, for garnish

Heat the water and oil in a large saucepan over medium heat. Add the onion and a pinch of the salt. Cook and stir for 5 minutes. Add the carrot and curry powder. Cook and stir for 3 minutes, or until the carrot is tender. Add the rice, mustard, remaining salt, and turmeric. Slowly add the broth and orange juice and bring to a boil over medium-high heat. Decrease the heat to low, cover, and simmer for 30 minutes.

Add the chickpeas and raisins, cover, and simmer for 15 minutes. Add the peas, cover, and simmer for 5 minutes longer.

Remove from the heat and let stand, covered, for 10 minutes. Transfer to a serving bowl and garnish with the cashews and cilantro. Serve hot.

Per serving: calories: 365, protein: 9 g, fat: 4 g, carbohydrate: 69 g, fiber: 7 g, sodium: 235 mg

Wild Rice Salad GLUTEN FREE

I tucked this recipe into the grain chapter despite wild rice's true identity as a wild grass. Regardless of its botanical family, it makes a dynamite salad.

Salad

2 cups vegetable broth

Pinch sea salt

1 cup wild rice, rinsed

½ cup roasted and sliced pecans

½ cup thinly sliced celery

⅓ cup fruit juice–sweetened dried cranberries

¼ cup minced red onion

¼ cup thinly sliced scallion

Dressing

¼ cup extra-virgin olive oil

Juice of 1 orange

2 tablespoons gluten-free brown rice syrup or maple syrup

2 teaspoons stone ground mustard

2 teaspoons brown rice vinegar or balsamic vinegar

2 teaspoons wheat-free tamari

To make the salad, put the broth and salt in a medium saucepan and bring to a boil over medium-high heat. Add the wild rice and stir. Cover, decrease the heat to medium-low, and simmer for 1 hour. Drain, if necessary, and set aside to cool.

Put the cooled wild rice, pecans, celery, cranberries, onion, and scallion in a large bowl.

To make the dressing, combine the dressing ingredients in a small saucepan. Whisk lightly and warm over low heat for about 5 minutes to allow the flavors to blend. Pour over the wild rice mixture and gently toss. Cover and chill in the refrigerator for 1 to 3 hours before serving.

Per serving: calories: 433, protein: 9 g, fat: 25 g, carbohydrate: 42 g, fiber: 6 g, sodium: 239 mg

Millet-Cauliflower Mash `GLUTEN FREE`

MAKES 4 SERVINGS

If you like mashed potatoes, you'll love this delicious alternative. The combination of nutritious millet and cauliflower make it a veritable powerhouse. Try smothering it with Mushroom Gravy (page 83) or Onion Gravy (page 82).

1 medium cauliflower, broken into florets (about 4 cups)

1 cup millet, rinsed

3½ cups vegetable broth

Sea salt

½ cup minced fresh parsley

2 teaspoons extra-virgin olive oil

Ground black pepper

Put the cauliflower and millet in a medium saucepan. Add the broth and a few pinches of salt. Bring to a boil over medium-high heat. Decrease the heat to low, cover, and simmer for 25 minutes, or until the cauliflower is fork-tender and the millet is fluffy.

Add the parsley and oil and mash with a potato masher. Season with pepper and additional salt to taste. Serve hot.

Per serving: calories: 308, protein: 11 g, fat: 5 g, carbohydrate: 49 g, fiber: 9 g, sodium: 114 mg

Mediterranean Barley Salad

The hardiest of all grains, barley is believed by some to be the most ancient grain cultivated by man. In this salad, the chewy texture of barley complements the crunch of refreshing watercress. Rich flavors from artichokes, fresh dill, and olives make this dish a winner at every gathering.

Salad

3½ cups water

1 cup pearl barley

Pinch sea salt

1 bunch fresh dill, minced (about 1 cup)

1 cup drained and quartered artichoke hearts (packed in water or oil)

1 cup chopped watercress

½ cup pitted kalamata olives

Dressing

2 tablespoons freshly squeezed lemon juice or balsamic vinegar

1 tablespoon extra-virgin olive oil

¼ teaspoon sea salt, or 1 tablespoon wheat-free tamari

To make the salad, put the water, barley, and salt in a medium saucepan and bring to a boil over medium-high heat. Decrease the heat to low, cover, and simmer for 1 hour, or until the barley is fluffy and tender. Transfer the barley to a large bowl to cool. When cool, add the dill, artichoke hearts, watercress, and olives.

To make the dressing, combine the lemon juice, oil, and salt in a small bowl and whisk until well blended. Pour over the barley mixture and gently toss until evenly distributed. Serve at room temperature or thoroughly chilled.

Per serving: calories: 262, protein: 7 g, fat: 7 g, carbohydrate: 34 g, fiber: 12 g, sodium: 293 mg

Basic Polenta GLUTEN FREE

Traditionally, corn was a dietary staple of the people of North and South America. Polenta is coarsely ground cornmeal that is cooked until soft and creamy, then served hot as a cereal or side dish, plain or topped with stir-fried vegetables. It may also be cooled (which causes it to firm up), sliced, and pan-fried. I sometimes add vegetables, such as grated carrot or corn kernels, to the polenta as it is cooking to give it a boost of flavor, color, texture, and nutrition.

4 to 5 cups vegetable broth or water

Pinch sea salt

1 cup yellow corn grits (polenta)

Bring the broth to a boil in a medium saucepan over medium-high heat. Add the salt. Slowly whisk in the corn grits, stirring constantly until the mixture boils. Decrease the heat to low, cover, and cook for 40 minutes, whisking occasionally to prevent lumping. Serve hot.

Per serving: calories: 168, protein: 6 g, fat: 2 g, carbohydrate: 28 g, fiber: 7 g, sodium: 108 mg

Polenta Slices: Cook the polenta as directed. Rinse an 8 x 8-inch glass baking dish with water (do not dry the dish) and pour the polenta into it. Smooth the top and cool at room temperature for 1 hour. Slice and serve with your favorite sauce. Alternatively, fry the slices in a small amount of oil until golden brown on both sides. Drain on paper towels and sprinkle lightly with sea salt.

Tempeh Mock Tuna Salad, page 67

Zucchini Rice Cakes with Vegan Tartar Sauce, pages 88-89

Three Bean Salad, page 112

Chili con Veggie, page 103

Sweet Potato–Polenta Pancakes GLUTEN FREE

MAKES 8 PANCAKES

These tasty pancakes will disappear as fast as you can make them.

2 cups water

½ cup yellow
   corn grits (polenta)

Sea salt

2 cups peeled and coarsely
   grated sweet potato

½ cup pecans, finely chopped

⅛ teaspoon ground nutmeg,
   plus more for garnish

Grapeseed oil or other oil,
   for frying

½ cup vegan sour cream

½ cup unsweetened
   applesauce

Bring the water to a boil in a medium saucepan over medium-high heat. Add a pinch of salt. Slowly whisk in the corn grits, stirring constantly until the mixture boils. Decrease the heat to low, cover, and cook for 30 minutes, whisking occasionally to prevent lumping. Stir in the sweet potato, pecans, and nutmeg, cover, and cook for 10 minutes longer. Remove from the heat, uncover, and let stand for 10 minutes to cool slightly.

Lightly oil a baking sheet. Spoon ½ cup of the polenta onto the baking sheet and flatten it with moistened fingers to form a patty. Repeat with the remaining polenta (there should be enough for 8 pancakes).

Heat ½ inch of oil in a cast iron skillet over medium heat. Fry a few pancakes at a time in the hot oil, browning each side. Drain on paper towels to remove the excess oil. Sprinkle lightly with salt. Serve hot, with a dollop of vegan sour cream, a dollop of applesauce, and a sprinkle of nutmeg.

Per serving: calories: 240, protein: 4 g, fat: 8 g, carbohydrate: 38 g, fiber: 5 g, sodium: 30 mg

Confetti Bulger GLUTEN FREE

MAKES 4 SERVINGS

Popular in Middle Eastern cooking, bulgur makes great pilafs and salads and is a featured ingredient in the well-known dish tabouli. If you can't have wheat, feel free to substitute rice couscous for the bulgur.

Salad

1⅓ cups water

Pinch sea salt

1 cup bulgur

½ cup fresh or thawed frozen corn kernels

½ cup frozen green peas

3 red radishes, cut in half and thinly sliced into half-moons

1 carrot, diced

2 stalks celery, diced

1 cup minced fresh parsley

½ cup walnuts, coarsely chopped

To make the salad, put the water and salt in a small saucepan and bring to a boil over medium-high heat. Add the bulgur, stir, cover, and decrease the heat to low. Cook for 20 minutes.

Put several inches of water in a medium saucepan and bring to a boil over medium-high heat. Drop the corn into the boiling water. After 1 minute, remove the corn with a fine-mesh skimmer and transfer it to a colander to cool and drain. Repeat this process with the peas, radishes, and carrot, boiling each type of vegetable separately. (Cook the stronger-tasting and more colorful vegetables last, so that each vegetable retains its distinctive flavor and hue.)

Remove the bulgur from the heat, fluff with a fork, and transfer to a large glass bowl to cool. Add the cooked vegetables, celery, parsley, and walnuts.

Dressing

2 tablespoons freshly squeezed orange juice

1 tablespoon brown rice vinegar or freshly squeezed lemon juice

1 tablespoon gluten-free brown rice syrup

2 teaspoons wheat-free tamari

1 teaspoon extra-virgin olive oil

To make the dressing, combine the orange juice, vinegar, syrup, tamari, and oil in a small bowl and whisk until well blended. Pour the dressing over the warm bulgur and vegetables and gently toss until evenly distributed. Serve at room temperature or thoroughly chilled.

Per serving: calories: 262, protein: 9 g, fat: 10 g, carbohydrate: 29 g, fiber: 10 g, sodium: 39 mg

Sunny Minted Quinoa `GLUTEN FREE`

Quinoa boasts the highest amount of protein compared to other grains. Native to South America, quinoa cooks up fluffy like a pilaf.

Salad

2 cups vegetable broth

1 cup quinoa, rinsed

⅓ cup sliced dried apricots

¼ cup chopped fresh mint leaves

Dressing

¼ cup freshly squeezed orange juice

2 tablespoons gluten-free brown rice syrup

1 tablespoon umeboshi vinegar

1 teaspoon extra-virgin olive oil or flax oil

½ cup thinly sliced scallions

⅓ cup toasted sunflower seeds

Sea salt

Ground black pepper

To make the salad, bring the broth to a boil in a medium saucepan over medium-high heat. Stir in the quinoa. Cover, decrease the heat to low, and simmer for 25 minutes, or until the quinoa has absorbed all the liquid. Fluff the quinoa with a fork and add the apricots and mint leaves.

To make the dressing, combine the orange juice, syrup, vinegar, and oil and whisk until well blended. Pour over the quinoa mixture. Add the scallions and sunflower seeds and mix gently. Season with salt and pepper to taste. Serve at room temperature or thoroughly chilled.

Per serving: calories: 325, protein: 10 g, fat: 11 g, carbohydrate: 42 g, fiber: 8 g, sodium: 837 mg

CHAPTER EIGHT

Savory Beans

I KNOW. YOU AND BEANS JUST DON'T GET ALONG. I hear this concern all the time. Don't worry, there's hope! Half the battle is knowing how to cook beans. The other half is eating them regularly so your body can adjust to the fiber content and begin to digest them better. In countries where beans are consumed regularly (such as Mexico and India), people have no problem digesting them. It's only when beans are consumed infrequently that we run into digestive issues. Beans are a terrific, delicious, low-fat source of protein, fiber, and many health-promoting vitamins and minerals.

Tips for Cooking Dried Beans

- Pick through dried beans to remove any small stones, debris, and odd-looking beans. Then rinse the beans thoroughly.

- Soak the beans in water to cover by several inches for 8 to 12 hours. (Lentils, mung beans, and split peas do not need to be soaked.)

- Discard the soaking water. Put the beans in a large pot and cover them with fresh water by several inches. Bring to a boil and boil uncovered for 10 minutes. Skim off any foam that accumulates at the surface.

- Add a small amount of cold water to the beans. The cold water "shocks" the beans and will make them softer.

- Cook the beans with bay leaves or a piece of kombu (a sea vegetable) to help make the beans more digestible.

- Partially cover the beans for the remainder of the cooking time, until they are tender, adding more water as necessary so they do not boil dry.

- Add sea salt only after the beans have softened.

- Use a pressure cooker for chickpeas and soybeans, as they are difficult to cook thoroughly otherwise.

If these tips do not result in super-soft beans, the beans you're using may be too old. In that case I recommend tossing them out and starting over with fresh beans. When beans have been sitting around too long, they get very dried out and will not become soft, even after adequate cooking.

Adzuki Beans and Squash GLUTEN FREE

MAKES 4 TO 6 SERVINGS

Long prized in Japan as a kidney tonic, adzuki beans have also been reputed to help regulate hypoglycemia when combined with squash, as in this recipe. This dish can even help tame cravings for sweets.

½ cup dried adzuki beans, sorted, rinsed, and soaked in water to cover for 8 to 12 hours

1 (1-inch) piece kombu, soaked in water for 10 minutes and drained

3 cups peeled and cubed winter squash (in 2-inch chunks)

¼ teaspoon sea salt

Drain the beans. Finely dice the kombu and put it in a medium saucepan. Put the squash on top of the kombu, and put the beans on top of the squash. Add enough fresh water to almost cover the squash and beans. Bring to a boil over medium-high heat. Decrease the heat to low, cover, and simmer for 1 hour, or until the beans and squash are soft. Add a little more water, if needed, to prevent the beans from cooking dry. Add the salt, cover, and cook for 15 minutes longer, or until most of the liquid has evaporated. Remove from the heat and let rest, covered, for 10 minutes before serving.

Per serving: calories: 92, protein: 5 g, fat: 1 g, carbohydrate: 14 g, fiber: 6 g, sodium: 136 mg

Chili con Veggie GLUTEN FREE

See photo facing page 97

MAKES 6 SERVINGS

According to an old American Indian legend, the first chili recipe was recorded on paper in the seventeenth century by a nun, Sister Mary of Agreda of Spain, known to the Indians as *La Dama de Azul*, the lady in blue. Ironically, Spanish priests during the nineteenth century warned against the aphrodisiac effects of chile peppers, and this likely inadvertently contributed to the popularity of chili.

1 tablespoon water

1 teaspoon grapeseed oil or other oil

1 cup diced onion

2 cloves minced garlic

Pinch sea salt

2 stalks celery, diced

2 carrots, diced

1 tablespoon finely minced beet

3 cups cooked or canned kidney or pinto beans, drained and rinsed

1 cup seitan, minced (optional)

2 teaspoons chili powder

½ teaspoon ground cumin

¼ teaspoon cayenne (optional)

4 cups vegetable broth or water

2 tablespoons kuzu starch, or 3 tablespoons arrowroot starch, mixed with ¼ cup water

1 tablespoon wheat-free tamari

1 tablespoon umeboshi vinegar

⅓ cup minced fresh cilantro, for garnish

Heat the water and oil in a soup pot over medium heat. Add the onion, garlic, and salt. Cook and stir for 5 minutes, or until the onion is translucent and tender. Add the celery, carrots, and beet. Cook and stir for 5 minutes. Stir in the beans, optional seitan, chili powder, cumin, and optional cayenne. Add the broth and bring to a boil over medium-high heat. Cover, decrease the heat to low, and simmer for 30 minutes.

Stir in the kuzu mixture, tamari, and vinegar. Stir until the chili thickens. Serve hot, garnished with the cilantro.

Per serving: calories: 180, protein: 10 g, fat: 2 g, carbohydrate: 23 g, fiber: 9 g, sodium: 766 mg

Simple Lentils with Veggies `GLUTEN FREE`

MAKES 4 SERVINGS

Lentils are said to be the oldest cultivated legume; lentil seeds have even been found in Egyptian tombs. Lentils are quick-cooking and are an excellent, low-fat source of protein and several vitamins and minerals.

1½ cups diced mixed vegetables (such as burdock root, cabbage, carrot, celery, corn kernels, leek, onion, parsnip, rutabaga, squash, or turnip)

1 cup dried lentils (any kind), sorted, rinsed, and drained

¼ teaspoon sea salt

¼ cup chopped scallion or fresh parsley, for garnish

Put the vegetables in a medium saucepan and put the lentils on top. Add enough water to cover the lentils, and bring to a boil over medium-high heat. Cover, decrease the heat to medium-low, and simmer for 30 minutes, or until the lentils are tender. Add a small amount of additional water during cooking to prevent the lentils from drying out.

Add the salt and cook for 10 minutes longer. Serve hot, garnished with the scallion.

Per serving: calories: 213, protein: 15 g, fat: 1 g, carbohydrate: 26 g, fiber: 13 g, sodium: 143 mg

Lentil-Walnut Pâté GLUTEN FREE

MAKES 4 SERVINGS

Lentils are a staple in Mediterranean, Middle Eastern, and Indian cuisine. These versatile little beans are well suited to dips, pâtés, patties, soups, and spreads; they can even be used to make a vegetarian meatloaf. This recipe is perfect for parties and entertaining. Serve it with crudités or whole-grain pita wedges.

2 cups cooked or canned lentils, drained and rinsed

½ cup walnuts

½ cup minced onion

½ cup minced fresh parsley

2 tablespoons balsamic vinegar

2 tablespoons gluten-free brown rice syrup

1 tablespoon sweet white miso

1 tablespoon wheat-free tamari

2 cloves minced garlic

Ground black pepper

Mirin, as needed (to achieve a smooth consistency)

Combine the lentils, walnuts, onion, parsley, vinegar, syrup, miso, tamari, garlic, and pepper to taste in a blender or food processor. Add just enough mirin to facilitate processing. Process until smooth. Stored in a sealed container in the refrigerator, Lentil-Walnut Pâté will keep for 4 days.

Per serving: calories: 263, protein: 13 g, fat: 10 g, carbohydrate: 24 g, fiber: 9 g, sodium: 343 mg

French Lentil Salad GLUTEN FREE

MAKES 6 SERVINGS

Oui, oui! These tiny little lentils hold their shape well and are perfect for this salad. You'll love the contrast of textures between the crunchy veggies and the tender French lentils.

2 cups dried French lentils, sorted, rinsed, and drained

1 (1-inch piece) kombu, soaked in water for 10 minutes and drained

½ teaspoon sea salt

¼ cup brown rice vinegar

2 tablespoons maple syrup or gluten-free brown rice syrup

1 tablespoon extra-virgin olive oil

1 tablespoon wheat-free tamari

2 stalks celery, diced

1 cup fresh or thawed frozen corn kernels, cooked and drained

1 cup chopped fresh parsley

½ cup diced red onion

⅓ cup finely diced carrot

Put the kombu in a medium saucepan. Put the lentils on top of the kombu and cover with water. Bring to a boil over medium-high heat and boil uncovered for 10 minutes. Add a little more water, if needed, to keep the lentils covered. Decrease the heat to medium-low, cover, and simmer for 30 minutes. Add the salt, cover, and simmer for 5 minutes longer, or until the liquid has evaporated.

Remove the kombu and either finely chop it and stir it back into the lentils or discard it. Transfer the cooked lentils to a large bowl to cool.

To make the dressing, combine the vinegar, syrup, oil, and tamari in a small bowl and whisk until well blended.

Add the celery, corn, parsley, onion, and carrot to the lentils. Pour the dressing over the lentil mixture and toss gently until evenly distributed. Cover and marinate in the refrigerator for at least 1 hour before serving. Stored in a sealed container in the refrigerator, French Lentil Salad will keep for 4 days.

Per serving: calories: 308, protein: 19 g, fat: 3 g, carbohydrate: 36 g, fiber: 17 g, sodium: 371 mg

Boston Baked Beans

Bring a batch of these babies to your next picnic and nobody will ever miss the ham hock or bacon.

1 (1-inch piece) kombu, soaked in water for 10 minutes and drained

2 cups dried navy beans, sorted, rinsed, and soaked in water to cover for 6 to 8 hours

2½ tablespoons grapeseed oil or other oil

8 strips tempeh bacon

2 tablespoons water

1 cup diced onion

1 cup unsweetened apple butter

¼ cup barley malt

2 tablespoons maple syrup

2 tablespoons yellow mustard

1 tablespoon wheat-free tamari

Mince the kombu and put it in a medium saucepan. Drain the beans and put them on top of the kombu. Add enough water to cover the beans. Bring to a boil over medium-high heat and boil uncovered for 10 minutes. Add a little more water, if needed, to keep the beans covered. Decrease the heat to low, cover, and simmer for 1 hour, or until the beans are soft. Drain and set aside to cool.

While the beans are cooking, heat 2 tablespoons of the oil in a cast iron skillet over medium heat. Add the tempeh bacon and fry until golden brown on both sides. Transfer to a plate lined with paper towels to absorb the excess oil. When cool to the touch, break the tempeh bacon into small pieces.

Put the remaining ½ tablespoon of oil and the 2 tablespoons of water in a large saucepan over medium heat. Add the onion and cook and stir for 5 minutes, or until tender. Add the beans, apple butter, barley malt, syrup, mustard, tamari, and tempeh bacon pieces. Cover and simmer on low heat for 30 minutes.

Preheat the oven to 350 degrees F. Lightly oil a 2-quart casserole. Spoon the bean mixture into the casserole, cover, and bake for 30 minutes. Serve hot or at room temperature.

Per serving: calories: 470, protein: 19 g, fat: 11 g, carbohydrate: 61 g, fiber: 17 g, sodium: 233 mg

Beans and Franks: Omit the tempeh bacon and the 2 tablespoons of oil. Add 1 cup of sliced vegan hot dogs along with the apple butter and seasonings.

Chickpeas with Carrot and Onion GLUTEN FREE

MAKES 4 SERVINGS

Sweet and rich-tasting, this simple dish can be transformed into a delicious spread the next day just by blending, mashing, or processing it.

1 (1-inch) piece kombu, soaked in water for 10 minutes and drained

1 cup dried chickpeas, sorted, rinsed, and soaked in water to cover for 8 to 12 hours

1 cup diced carrot

1 cup diced onion

¼ teaspoon sea salt

¼ cup chopped scallion or fresh parsley, for garnish

Finely mince the kombu and put it in a medium pressure cooker or saucepan. Drain the chickpeas and put them on top of the kombu. Add enough water to cover the chickpeas, and bring to a boil over high heat, skimming off the foam that accumulates at the surface. Boil for 10 minutes, continuing to remove any foam. Add a little more water, if needed, to keep the chickpeas covered.

To pressure cook, lock the cover in place and bring the cooker up to full pressure over medium-high heat. Once the cooker is at full pressure, decrease the heat to low and cook for 50 minutes. Remove from the heat and let the pressure drop naturally. When the pressure is fully released, open the cooker and transfer the chickpeas to a medium bowl. Put the carrot and onion in the cooker. Put the chickpeas on top of the vegetables and add the remaining cooking liquid. If no cooking liquid remains, add ½ cup of water to the cooker. Cover the cooker but do not lock the lid, and bring to a boil over medium-high heat. Decrease the heat to low and simmer for 30 minutes.

To cook the chickpeas in a saucepan, after they have boiled for 10 minutes, decrease the heat to low, partially cover, and simmer for 2 hours, or until the beans are soft, adding more water as needed to keep the chickpeas covered. Transfer the chickpeas to a medium bowl. Put the carrot and onion in the saucepan. Put the chickpeas on top of the vegetables and add the remaining cooking liquid. If no cooking liquid remains, add ½ cup of water to the saucepan. Bring to a boil over medium-high heat. Decrease the heat to low, cover, and simmer for 30 minutes.

Add the salt, cover, and cook for 10 minutes longer, or until the beans and vegetables are soft and the liquid has evaporated. Transfer to a serving dish. Serve hot, garnished with the scallion.

Per serving: calories: 100, protein: 4 g, fat: 1 g, carbohydrate: 14 g, fiber: 5 g, sodium: 186 mg

Black Soybeans with Carrot and Onion: Replace the chickpeas with an equal amount of dried black soybeans (the cooking time will be the same). Use 1 to 2 teaspoons of wheat-free tamari instead of sea salt. Add ½ teaspoon of ginger juice the last few minutes of cooking.

Kidney Bean Salad

MAKES 6 SERVINGS

True to their namesake, these dark red beans are shaped like kidneys. They are used to make chili, red beans and rice, and savory bean salads like this one.

Salad

1 (1-inch) piece kombu, soaked in water for 10 minutes and drained

2 cups dried kidney beans, sorted, rinsed, and soaked in water to cover for 6 to 8 hours

1 cup cauliflower florets

1 small zucchini, cut in half lengthwise and sliced into half-moons

1 cup fresh or frozen corn kernels or frozen lima beans

⅓ cup chopped fresh parsley

To make the salad, put the kombu in a medium saucepan. Drain the beans and put them on top of the kombu. Add enough water to cover the beans, and bring to a boil over medium-high heat, skimming off any foam that accumulates at the surface. Boil uncovered for 10 minutes, continuing to remove any foam. Add a little more water, if needed, to keep the beans covered. Decrease the heat to low, cover, and cook for 1 hour, or until the beans are tender. Drain and transfer the beans to a large glass bowl to cool.

In a separate saucepan, bring several inches of water to a boil over medium-high heat. Add the cauliflower and blanch it for 2 minutes. Transfer the cauliflower to a colander with a slotted spoon. Rinse the cauliflower under cold water and drain. Repeat this process with the zucchini and corn. Add the blanched vegetables and parsley to the beans.

Dressing

Juice of 1 orange

2 tablespoons balsamic vinegar

2 tablespoons maple syrup

1 tablespoon wheat-free tamari

2 teaspoons horseradish mustard

2 teaspoons sesame oil

To make the dressing, combine all the ingredients in a small bowl and whisk until well blended. Pour over the bean mixture and stir gently until evenly distributed. Cover and marinate in the refrigerator at least 1 hour before serving. Stored in a sealed container in the refrigerator, Kidney Bean Salad will keep for 4 days.

Per serving: calories: 224, protein: 12 g, fat: 2 g, carbohydrate: 32 g, fiber: 9 g, sodium: 196 mg

Three Bean Salad   GLUTEN FREE

See photo between pages 96-97

MAKES 4 TO 6 SERVINGS

Why choose just one bean when you can have three? This classic salad will leave you with an empty bowl when you serve it at family gatherings.

Dressing

½ cup minced red onion

3 tablespoons gluten-free brown rice syrup or maple syrup

3 tablespoons brown rice vinegar

2 tablespoons stone ground mustard

1 tablespoon extra-virgin olive oil

1 tablespoon wheat-free tamari

Salad

2 cups trimmed and cut fresh green beans (in 2-inch pieces)

2 cups cooked or canned chickpeas, drained and rinsed

2 cups cooked or canned great northern beans, drained and rinsed

2 cups cooked or canned kidney beans, drained and rinsed

½ cup minced fresh dill

To make the dressing, put the onion in a small glass bowl. Combine the syrup, vinegar, mustard, oil, and tamari in a separate small glass bowl and whisk until well blended. Pour over the onion, stir well, and set aside.

To make the salad, put a couple of inches of water in a medium saucepan. Add the green beans and bring to a boil over high heat. Decrease the heat to medium, cover, and cook for 5 minutes, or until the green beans are tender. Drain the green beans in a colander or strainer and rinse them under cold water. Transfer to a large bowl and add the chickpeas, great northern beans, kidney beans, and dill. Add the dressing mixture and toss until evenly distributed. Cover and refrigerate the salad for at least 1 hour before serving. Stored in a sealed container in the refrigerator, Three Bean Salad will keep for 4 days.

Per serving: calories: 354, protein: 19 g, fat: 5 g, carbohydrate: 44 g, fiber: 16 g, sodium: 255 mg

White Beans and Greens GLUTEN FREE

When I was just a wee tyké, my grandfather, Vincenzo Agresta from Calabria, Italy, prepared sautéed beans and greens regularly, much to my delight. This is my version of beans and greens, dedicated to Grandpa Agresta.

2 tablespoons water

1 teaspoon extra-virgin olive oil

1 small onion, diced

2 garlic cloves, minced (2 teaspoons)

3 cups cooked or canned cannellini beans or great northern beans, drained and rinsed

5 cups chopped kale

Sea salt

Ground black pepper

Heat the water and oil in a large skillet over medium heat. Add the onion and garlic and cook and stir for 5 minutes, or until the onion is translucent and soft. Add the beans and cook and stir for 5 minutes. Add the kale and a splash of additional water, if needed, to keep the beans from sticking to the skillet. Season with salt and pepper to taste. Cover and cook for 5 to 10 minutes, or until the kale has wilted and is tender to your liking. Serve hot or at room temperature.

Per serving: calories: 216, protein: 14 g, fat: 2 g, carbohydrate: 27 g, fiber: 11 g, sodium: 40 mg

THE NATURAL VEGAN KITCHEN   113

Creamy Black Beans with Squash and Onion GLUTEN FREE

Black beans have an earthy flavor and rich texture. They are especially soothing and satisfying paired with winter squash, which provides a beautiful contrast of color. This dish makes a splendid stuffing for burritos.

1 (1-inch) piece kombu, soaked in water for 10 minutes and drained

1 cup dried black turtle beans, sorted, rinsed, and soaked in water to cover for 8 to 12 hours

1 cup peeled and cubed winter squash

1 cup diced onion

1 cup grated brown rice mochi

2 teaspoons wheat-free tamari

1 teaspoon ground cumin

¼ teaspoon sea salt

½ cup thinly sliced scallions, for garnish

Mince the kombu and put it in a medium saucepan. Drain the beans and put them on top of the kombu. Add enough water to cover the beans. Bring to a boil, skimming off any foam that accumulates at the surface. Boil uncovered for 10 minutes, continuing to remove any foam. Add a little more water, if needed, to keep the beans covered. Decrease the heat to low, cover, and simmer for 1 hour, or until the beans are soft. Drain and transfer to a medium glass bowl.

Put the squash and onion in the same saucepan used to cook the beans. Add the beans (and any bean cooking liquid) on top. Add ¼ cup of water if the mixture is too thick to be easily stirred. Bring to a boil over medium-high heat. Decrease the heat to low, cover, and simmer for 20 minutes, or until the beans and the vegetables are tender. Stir in the mochi, tamari, cumin, and salt. Cover and cook for 10 minutes, or until the mochi melts. Transfer the mixture to a serving dish. Serve hot, garnished with the scallions.

Per serving: calories: 251, protein: 13 g, fat: 1 g, carbohydrate: 37 g, fiber: 13 g, sodium: 316 mg

CHAPTER NINE

The Main Dish and Casserole City

WHEN I WANT TO WOW SOMEONE WITH NATURAL VEGAN COOKING, I whip up a delicious, hearty main dish or casserole. When you're in the mood for comfort food, nothing cuts it like Fried Seitan Nuggets (page 126) or Vegetarian Sloppy Joes (page 121). Soyfoods like tofu and tempeh (a fermented product that originated in Indonesia) make these types of recipes possible.

Seitan (pronounced say-tahn) is another key ingredient in making hearty main dishes. What is seitan? Let's just say it has nothing to do with the devil, but it does pack lots of protein and essential amino acids in every holy morsel. Seitan provides, ounce for ounce, as much protein as a steak, minus the cholesterol, calories, and saturated fat. If you tend to crave meaty textures that you can sink your teeth into, search no further. I've served many seitan dishes that caused worried vegetarians to ask, "Are you sure this isn't meat?"

Noodles are another one of my secret-weapon ingredients. The joy of slurping noodles is universal. It's no wonder they're such a hit with kids of all ages. Select whole-grain pasta over products made from refined flours to ramp up the nutrients, lower the calories, and add extra flavor. Stick with wholesome varieties made from brown rice, buckwheat, corn, quinoa, spelt, or whole wheat.

Tofu Quiche GLUTEN FREE

MAKES 8 SERVINGS

Real men *do* eat quiche—tofu quiche, that is! Nobody can resist a slice of this savory dish, brimming with fresh veggies.

- 1 pound firm tofu, drained
- 2 tablespoons water
- 1 teaspoon grapeseed oil or other oil
- 2 cups button mushrooms, thinly sliced
- 1 teaspoon dried basil
- ½ teaspoon dried oregano
- ½ teaspoon sea salt
- ½ cup diced carrot
- ½ cup thinly sliced leek
- ½ cup broccoli florets
- Ground black pepper
- 2 teaspoons sweet white miso
- 1 teaspoon umeboshi vinegar
- ¼ teaspoon ground turmeric
- 1 (9-inch) whole-grain pie crust, prebaked for 5 minutes at 350 degrees F (optional)

Preheat the oven to 350 degrees F.

Put the tofu in a colander in the sink and put a few small plates on top of it. Let the water drain from the tofu for 10 minutes.

Heat 1 tablespoon of the water and the oil in a medium skillet over medium heat. Add the mushrooms, basil, oregano, and a pinch of the salt. Cover and cook for 5 minutes, or until the mushrooms have softened. Add the carrot and leek and cook and stir for 5 minutes. Add the broccoli and pepper to taste. Cook and stir for about 5 minutes, until the vegetables are just tender (do not overcook them). Add a small splash of water, if needed, to keep the vegetables from sticking to the skillet.

Crumble the tofu into a food processor. Add the miso, vinegar, remaining salt, and turmeric. Process until smooth. Transfer to a bowl and fold in the cooked vegetables. Pour into the pie crust, if using, or into a lightly oiled 9-inch pie plate. Bake for 1 hour. Let stand for at least 30 minutes before slicing and serving. Covered and stored in the refrigerator, Tofu Quiche will keep for 4 days.

Per serving: calories: 214, protein: 9 g, fat: 13 g, carbohydrate: 14 g, fiber: 2 g, sodium: 431 mg

Tofu Lasagne `GLUTEN FREE`

Mama mia! You'll never miss the cheese in this delicious tofu-based version of lasagne. If you don't have the time to make the Carrot-Beet Marinara Sauce, use your favorite tomato sauce instead.

1½ pounds firm tofu, drained

2 tablespoons sweet white miso

6 cups Carrot-Beet Marinara Sauce (page 80) or tomato sauce

1 (10-ounce) package whole-grain or gluten-free lasagne noodles, cooked in boiling water until al dente and drained

3 cups grated brown rice mochi (see note)

6 cups chopped kale, steamed and drained (optional)

Preheat the oven to 350 degrees F. Lightly rub the bottom and sides of a 9 x 12-inch glass lasagne pan with extra-virgin olive oil.

Put the tofu in a colander in the sink and put a few small plates on top of it. Let the water drain from the tofu for 10 minutes. Crumble the tofu into a bowl. Add the miso and mash with a fork to mix well. Set aside.

Spread a few tablespoons of the sauce over the bottom of the prepared pan. Arrange a layer of the noodles on top of the sauce. Spread with half of the tofu mixture. Sprinkle evenly with half of the mochi. Distribute half of the kale, if using, over the mochi. Spoon a thin layer of sauce evenly over the kale (or mochi, if not using the kale). Repeat the layers, ending with a layer of the noodles topped with the remaining sauce.

Cover the lasagne with foil and bake for 40 minutes. Remove the cover and bake for 10 minutes longer, or until bubbly. Cool for 15 minutes before slicing and serving.

Note: A food processor fitted with the grating blade will make grating the mochi easy and fast.

Per serving: calories: 453, protein: 15 g, fat: 8 g, carbohydrate: 76 g, fiber: 5 g, sodium: 806 mg

Rainbow Noodles GLUTEN FREE

This colorful and easy-to-make dish creates a striking presentation. The rainbow of colorful vegetables provides a broad spectrum of vitamins and antioxidants.

2 tablespoons water

1 teaspoon sesame oil

½ red onion, thinly sliced into half-moons

2 cloves garlic, minced (2 teaspoons)

1 teaspoon peeled and minced fresh ginger

Sea salt

½ cup thinly sliced red cabbage

½ cup carrot matchsticks

8 ounces whole-grain or gluten-free noodles, cooked according to the package directions

Heat the water and oil in a large skillet over medium heat. Add the onion, garlic, ginger, and a pinch of salt. Cook and stir for 3 minutes. Add the cabbage and carrot and cook and stir for 1 minute. Add the noodles, broccoli, optional tofu, corn, tamari, syrup, and vinegar. Stir gently. (I like to use bamboo cooking chopsticks for this.) Cover and cook for 5 to 7 minutes longer, or until all the vegetables are tender but still brightly colored. Serve hot, garnished with the parsley.

1 cup broccoli spears

1 cup cubed ready-made baked marinated tofu (see note; optional)

½ cup fresh or frozen corn kernels

1 tablespoon wheat-free tamari

2 teaspoons gluten-free brown rice syrup or maple syrup

2 teaspoons brown rice vinegar

¼ cup chopped fresh parsley

Note: To make homemade baked marinated tofu, preheat the oven to 350 degrees F. Slice 14 ounces of firm or extra-firm tofu into bite-sized cubes. Spread the cubes in a single layer on a baking sheet and sprinkle them evenly with 1 tablespoon of wheat-free tamari. Bake for 30 minutes, carefully turning the cubes over after 15 minutes.

Per serving: calories: 303, protein: 15 g, fat: 5 g, carbohydrate: 52 g, fiber: 9 g, sodium: 383 mg

Fettuccine with Chickpeas, Corn, and Kale GLUTEN FREE

MAKES 4 SERVINGS

Simple, elegant, and light, this dish makes a perfect summer meal.

14 ounces brown rice fettuccine, cooked according to package directions

1 cup cooked or canned chickpeas, drained and rinsed

1 cup fresh or frozen corn kernels, cooked and drained

⅓ cup minced fresh chives

1 bunch kale, washed, stemmed, and torn into bite-sized pieces (about 6 cups)

2 tablespoons extra-virgin olive oil or flax oil

2 tablespoons toasted sesame seeds

1 tablespoon wheat-free tamari

1 tablespoon brown rice vinegar

1 teaspoon maple syrup

1 teaspoon mustard (any kind)

Combine the fettuccine, chickpeas, corn, and chives in a large bowl.

Steam the kale in a steamer basket over boiling water for 5 minutes, or until the kale is bright green and tender. Transfer to a medium bowl.

Combine the oil, sesame seeds, tamari, vinegar, syrup, and mustard in a small bowl and whisk until well blended. Drizzle over the fettuccine mixture and toss gently until evenly distributed. Transfer to a large serving bowl. Arrange the kale around the edges of the fettuccine to form a wreath. Serve at once.

Per serving: calories: 598, protein: 18 g, fat: 12 g, carbohydrate: 103 g, fiber: 7 g, sodium: 301 mg

Vegetarian Sloppy Joes

Tempeh, like tofu, is a chameleon food. It absorbs the flavors it's cooked with, and you can season it to taste just like your old family favorites. You're sure to love it in this recipe.

1 (8-ounce) package gluten-free tempeh

2 tablespoons water

1 teaspoon sesame oil

1 cup diced onion

2 cloves minced garlic (2 teaspoons)

Pinch sea salt

1 cup unsweetened apple butter

1 tablespoon wheat-free tamari

2 teaspoons stone ground mustard

4 whole-grain buns

Steam the tempeh in a steamer basket over boiling water for 15 minutes. Transfer to a plate to cool. When the tempeh is cool enough to handle, coarsely grate it or crumble it by hand into a medium bowl.

Heat the water and oil in a large skillet over medium heat. Add the onion, garlic, and salt. Cook and stir for 10 minutes, or until the onion is translucent. Add the tempeh and cook and stir for 5 minutes.

Combine the apple butter, tamari, and mustard in a small bowl. Add to the tempeh and mix well. Cover and simmer for 10 minutes. Serve on whole-grain buns.

Per serving: calories: 423, protein: 16 g, fat: 12 g, carbohydrate: 59 g, fiber: 7 g, sodium: 458 mg

Tempeh Tacos `GLUTEN FREE`

MAKES 12 TACOS

Everyone loves tacos, and this version is no exception. The chewiness of tempeh makes a hearty filling you can really sink your teeth into.

Tempeh Filling

1 (8-ounce) package gluten-free tempeh

1 cup plus 2 tablespoons water

Juice of 2 limes

2 teaspoons wheat-free tamari

1 teaspoon chili powder

1 teaspoon ground cumin

Dash cayenne

1 teaspoon sesame oil

1 cup diced onion

2 cloves garlic, minced (2 teaspoons)

Pinch sea salt

12 taco shells, or 12 whole-grain tortillas (for soft tacos)

Topping Options

Shredded lettuce

Salsa

Guacamole

Tofu sour cream

To make the filling, steam the tempeh in a steamer basket over boiling water for 15 minutes. Transfer the tempeh to a plate to cool. When the tempeh is cool enough to handle, coarsely grate it or crumble it by hand into a medium bowl. Add 1 cup of the water and the lime juice, tamari, chili powder, cumin, and cayenne. Mix with a fork to gently combine.

Heat the remaining 2 tablespoons of water and the oil in a large skillet over medium heat. Add the onion, garlic, and salt. Cook and stir for 5 minutes, or until the onion is tender. Add a small amount of water, if needed, to prevent sticking.

Add the tempeh mixture and cook for about 15 minutes, or until the liquid has evaporated.

If using taco shells, preheat the oven to 350 degrees F. Arrange the taco shells on a baking sheet and warm them in the oven for 5 minutes. If using tortillas, preheat the oven to 250 degrees F. Stack the tortillas and wrap them in a damp dish towel. Put the wrapped stack in a casserole, cover, and warm in the oven for 20 minutes, then transfer to a tortilla warmer to keep hot. Stuff the warm taco shells or tortillas with the tempeh filling and add the toppings of your choice. Enjoy!

Per serving: calories: 107, protein: 5 g, fat: 5 g, carbohydrate: 10 g, fiber: 2 g, sodium: 103 mg

Tempeh Scramble `GLUTEN FREE`

This recipe includes watercress, a nutritional superfood with zippy, peppery leaves that can be found year-round. Look for watercress that is fresh, healthy, and deep green.

1 (8-ounce) package
gluten-free tempeh

2 tablespoons water

1 teaspoon grapeseed oil
or other oil

1 cup diced red onion

2 cloves garlic, minced
(2 teaspoons)

Pinch sea salt

2 cups diced carrots

1½ cups diced celery

½ cup vegetable broth

2 teaspoons yellow mustard

½ teaspoon umeboshi
plum paste

2 cups chopped
watercress leaves

½ cup chopped fresh basil

Steam the tempeh in a steamer basket over boiling water for 15 minutes. Transfer to a plate to cool. When the tempeh is cool enough to handle, cut it into ½-inch cubes.

Heat the water and oil in a medium skillet over medium heat. Add the onion, garlic, and salt. Cook and stir for 5 minutes. Add the carrots and celery and a small splash of water, if needed, to prevent sticking. Cook and stir for 5 minutes, or until the vegetables are tender.

Put the tempeh on top of the vegetables and add the broth. Cover and simmer over medium heat for 10 minutes, or until most of the broth has evaporated. Gently stir in the mustard and umeboshi plum paste. Add a little more water, if needed, to prevent sticking.

Stir in the watercress and basil and cook for 5 to 7 minutes longer, just until the watercress wilts. Serve hot.

Per serving: calories: 181, protein: 13 g, fat: 8 g, carbohydrate: 12g, fiber: 7 g, sodium: 405 mg

Baked Tempeh Kabobs GLUTEN FREE

MAKES 12 KABOBS

Who could resist a skewer loaded with juicy marinated veggies and chewy morsels of tempeh?

Kabobs

2 (8-ounce) packages gluten-free tempeh

4 cups bite-sized vegetable pieces (such as cherry tomatoes, colorful bell peppers, mushrooms, red onion, yellow squash, or zucchini)

To make the kabobs, steam the tempeh in a steamer basket over boiling water for 15 minutes. Transfer to a plate to cool. When the tempeh is cool enough to handle, cut it into 1-inch cubes.

To make the marinade, combine all the marinade ingredients in a small bowl and whisk until well blended. Put the tempeh in a glass storage container with a lid. Pour the marinade over the tempeh and stir gently to combine. Cover and refrigerate for 2 hours, occasionally stirring the tempeh to make sure the marinade evenly coats each piece.

Preheat a grill or the oven to 400 degrees F. Have ready 12 metal or bamboo skewers (see note).

Orange-Teriyaki Marinade

- ½ cup all-fruit orange marmalade or apricot preserves
- ½ cup freshly squeezed orange juice
- ¼ cup freshly squeezed lime juice
- 2 tablespoons wheat-free tamari
- 2 tablespoons gluten-free brown rice syrup
- 1 tablespoon grapeseed oil or other oil
- 1 tablespoon yellow mustard
- 1 tablespoon gluten-free vegan worcestershire sauce
- 2 cloves garlic, crushed (2 teaspoons)
- 1 teaspoon peeled and minced fresh ginger
- ½ teaspoon ground black pepper

Thread each skewer, alternating the vegetables and tempeh cubes. Reserve any extra marinade. Place the skewers in a single layer on a baking sheet. Brush or drizzle them evenly with the remaining marinade. Grill or bake the skewers for 10 to 15 minutes, until the vegetables and tempeh are evenly browned. Transfer the skewers to a serving platter. Serve hot.

Note: If using bamboo skewers, soak them in water for 1 hour before threading them.

Per serving: calories: 135, protein: 8 g, fat: 5 g, carbohydrate: 13 g, fiber: 3 g, sodium: 102 mg

Fried Seitan Nuggets

MAKES 6 SERVINGS

These little nuggets are devilishly good. If you have a wheat allergy or are gluten intolerant, substitute firm tofu that has been frozen and thawed (to give it a chewy texture), and replace the whole wheat pastry flour with any gluten-free flour of your choice.

Batter

½ cup whole wheat
    pastry flour

½ cup corn flour

2 tablespoons minced
    fresh parsley

⅛ teaspoon sea salt

1 cup cold water

2 teaspoons kuzu starch,
    or 3 teaspoons arrowroot
    starch, mixed with 1/4 cup
    cold water

1 tablespoon stone
    ground mustard

Nuggets

4 cups grapeseed oil
    or other oil, for frying

4 cups crispy brown rice cereal,
    crushed in a blender

1 cup whole wheat pastry flour

2 cups bite-sized seitan pieces

To make the batter, combine the pastry flour, corn flour, parsley, and salt in a medium mixing bowl. In a small glass bowl, combine the water, kuzu mixture, and mustard. Whisk until well blended. Add to the flour mixture and mix well.

To make the nuggets, heat 2 to 3 inches of the oil in a medium frying pan over medium-high heat. Put the crushed cereal and flour in separate bowls. Dip a piece of seitan into the flour and then into the batter. Finish with a coating of the cereal. Set the nugget on a plate and repeat this process with the remaining seitan.

Drop a few nuggets into the hot oil and fry for about 5 minutes, until the nuggets are golden brown and crispy. Transfer to a plate covered with several paper towels to absorb the excess oil. Repeat with the remaining nuggets until all are fried.

Barbecue Dipping Sauce

1 cup unsweetened apple butter

2 tablespoons wheat-free tamari

2 tablespoons maple syrup

1 tablespoon yellow mustard

Few dashes ground black pepper

To make the dipping sauce, combine all the sauce ingredients in a small saucepan and gently warm over low heat. Serve the hot nuggets with the warm dipping sauce on the side.

Per serving: calories: 830, protein: 30 g, fat: 39 g, carbohydrate: 82 g, fiber: 10 g, sodium: 531 mg

Three Sisters Casserole `GLUTEN FREE`

MAKES 6 SERVINGS

The American Indians formed legends around a trio of plants that sustained life for them. Squash, beans, and corn were planted together and known as the Three Sisters.

In late spring, we plant the corn and beans and squash. They're not just plants—we call them the three sisters. We plant them together, three kinds of seeds in one hole. They want to be together with each other, just as we Indians want to be together with each other. So long as the three sisters are with us we know we will never starve. The Creator sends them to us each year. We celebrate them now. We thank Him for the gift He gives us today and every day.

—**Chief Louis Farmer** (Onondaga)

6 cups vegetable broth

1½ cups yellow corn grits (polenta)

Sea salt

1 teaspoon sesame oil

2 tablespoons water

1 cup diced onion

1 cup diced carrot

½ cup diced celery

⅓ cup diced red bell pepper

1 teaspoon ground cumin

2 cups peeled and cubed winter squash

2 cups cooked or canned pinto beans, drained and rinsed

Preheat the oven to 350 degrees F. Coat a 9 x 12-inch glass baking dish with some of the oil.

Pour 4 cups of the broth into a medium saucepan and bring to a boil over medium-high heat. Add the corn grits and a pinch of salt, stirring constantly with a whisk to prevent lumping. Cover, reduce the heat to low, and simmer for 40 minutes, whisking occasionally, until the mixture is thick and creamy.

Pour half of the polenta into the prepared baking dish and set aside. Cover the remaining polenta to keep it warm.

Heat the remaining oil and the water in a large skillet over medium heat. Add the onion and a pinch of salt. Cook and stir for 5 minutes, or until the onion is translucent. Add the carrot, celery, bell pepper, cumin, and another pinch of salt. Cook and stir for 5 minutes, adding a small amount of water, as needed, to prevent sticking. Add the squash and the remaining 2 cups of broth. Bring to a boil over medium-high heat. Decrease the heat to low, cover, and simmer for 15 minutes, or until the squash is tender. Add the beans, corn, syrup, tamari, and vinegar and simmer for 5 minutes.

- **1 cup fresh or thawed frozen corn kernels**

- **2 tablespoons maple syrup**

- **2 teaspoons wheat-free tamari**

- **2 teaspoons umeboshi vinegar**

- **2 tablespoons kuzu starch, mixed with 1/4 cup cold water**

- **1/4 cup chopped fresh parsley, for garnish**

Slowly add the kuzu mixture, stirring constantly. Cook for 2 minutes longer, or until the mixture has thickened. Pour over the polenta in the baking dish. Spoon the remaining polenta evenly on top. Bake for 30 minutes. Cool for 10 minutes before cutting into squares. Serve hot, garnished with the parsley.

Per serving: calories: 364, protein: 13 g, fat: 4 g, carbohydrate: 59 g, fiber: 17 g, sodium: 573 mg

Tofu Pot Pie `GLUTEN FREE`

MAKES 6 SERVINGS

Mmm . . . comfort food to the max: steaming, gravy-laden vegetables encased in a golden pie crust.

Filling

2 tablespoons water

1 teaspoon grapeseed oil or other oil

1 cup diced onion

1/4 teaspoon sea salt

2 cups button mushrooms, cleaned and quartered

1 teaspoons dried thyme

1/2 teaspoon dried sage

1 cup thinly sliced carrot

1 cup sliced celery

1 cup peeled and diced rutabaga or diced turnip

1/2 cup green peas

1 1/2 cups vegetable broth

1 cup extra-firm tofu, drained and cubed

2 tablespoons wheat-free tamari

2 tablespoons kuzu starch, mixed with 1/4 cup cold water

Preheat the oven to 350 degrees F.

To make the filling, heat the water and oil in a large skillet over medium heat. Add the onion and a pinch of the salt. Cook and stir for 5 minutes. Add the mushrooms, thyme, sage, and another pinch of salt. Cook and stir for 5 minutes. Add the carrot, celery, rutabaga, peas, and another pinch of salt. Cook and stir for 5 minutes, adding a splash of water, if needed, to keep the vegetables from sticking to the skillet. Stir in the broth, tofu, and tamari. Add the kuzu mixture, stirring constantly until thickened. Remove from the heat to cool.

Crust

**2 cups whole wheat pastry
flour, or 2 cups gluten-free
flour plus ½ teaspoon
xanthan gum**

½ teaspoon sea salt

**⅓ cup grapeseed oil
or other oil**

½ cup ice water

To make the crust, combine the flour and salt in a large bowl.
Add the oil and mix it in with a fork. Gradually add the ice
water, 1 tablespoon at a time, adding just enough to bind the
dough. Divide the dough in half and shape it into 2 balls. Roll
each ball between 2 sheets of waxed or parchment paper to
create two 9-inch circles.

Line a glass pie plate with 1 circle of the dough. Pour the
vegetable mixture into the pie plate, cover with the remaining
circle of dough, and crimp the edges. Make several slits in the
top crust or cut out a few leaf shapes to vent the pie. Bake for
40 minutes, or until the crust is golden and the vegetables are
fork-tender.

Per serving: calories: 354, protein: 14 g, fat: 16 g, carbohydrate: 35 g,
fiber: 9 g, sodium: 625 mg

Neptune's Casserole GLUTEN FREE

MAKES 4 SERVINGS

Mom used to make a version of this rich, creamy casserole. A few crunchy dill pickles, served on the side, perfectly complement the flavors of this dish.

1 cup thin, bite-sized slices
  gluten-free tempeh

1 cup plus 2 tablespoons water

2 tablespoons freshly
  squeezed lemon juice

1 teaspoon wheat-free tamari

1 teaspoon grapeseed oil
  or other oil

3 cups thinly sliced
  button mushrooms

½ teaspoon sea salt

1 cup diced onion

½ cup diced celery

Preheat the oven to 350 degrees F. Oil a 9 x 12-inch glass casserole.

Steam the tempeh in a steamer basket over boiling water for 10 minutes. Transfer the tempeh to a medium saucepan. Add 1 cup of the water and 2 teaspoons of the lemon juice. Bring to a boil over medium-high heat. Decrease the heat to medium-low and simmer for 20 minutes, or until the liquid has evaporated. If the liquid has not fully evaporated after 20 minutes, increase the heat and continue cooking until it has. Set aside.

While the tempeh is simmering, heat the remaining 2 tablespoons of water and the oil in a separate medium saucepan. Add the mushrooms and a pinch of the salt. Cook and stir until the mushrooms have softened, about 5 minutes. Add the onion, celery, and another pinch of the salt. Cook and stir for about 8 minutes, or until all of the vegetables are tender. Slowly stir in the rice milk, the remaining salt, and pepper to taste. Gradually bring to a boil over medium heat, taking care that the mixture doesn't boil over. Decrease the heat to medium-low and cook, stirring occasionally, for 20 minutes.

4 cups plain rice milk

Ground black pepper

1 cup long-grain brown rice, rinsed

1½ cups fresh or frozen green peas

1 teaspoon paprika

¼ cup chopped fresh parsley

1 lemon, thinly sliced

4 dill pickles

Pour half of the mushroom mixture into the prepared casserole. Add the rice, peas, and reserved tempeh. Add the remaining mushroom mixture. Sprinkle with the remaining lemon juice and ½ teaspoon of the paprika. Cover and bake for 90 minutes, stirring once or twice during baking.

Garnish with the remaining paprika, parsley, and lemon slices. Serve hot, with the pickles on the side.

Per serving: calories: 478, protein: 19 g, fat: 10 g, carbohydrate: 78 g, fiber: 10 g, sodium: 580 mg

Enchilada Casserole GLUTEN FREE

MAKES 6 TO 8 SERVINGS

Who needs cheese to make a killer enchilada casserole! This vegan version rivals any traditional recipe.

1 cup vegetable broth

1 cup diced onion

2 cloves minced garlic (2 teaspoons)

1 teaspoon ground cumin

½ teaspoon sea salt

1 cup fresh or frozen corn kernels

Preheat the oven to 350 degrees F. Lightly oil a 9 x 13-inch glass lasagne pan with oil.

To make the onion sauce, put 2 tablespoons of the broth in a large skillet over medium heat. Add onion, garlic, cumin, and a pinch of the salt. Cook and stir for 5 minutes. Add the corn, olives, bell pepper, chili powder, cayenne, and another splash of the broth. Cook and stir for an 10 minutes. Add the remaining broth, salsa, carrot juice, and remaining salt and simmer for 3 minutes.

Put 6 of the tortillas on the bottom of the prepared pan, covering the entire surface. Spread half of the beans evenly over the tortillas. Cover the beans with one-third of the onion sauce. Add another layer of 6 tortillas. Top that layer with the remaining beans and half of the remaining onion sauce. Cover with the final 6 tortillas. Spread them with the remaining portion of the onion sauce.

1 cup coarsely chopped black olives (preferably kalamata)

½ cup diced green bell pepper

1½ teaspoons chili powder

¼ teaspoon cayenne

2 cups salsa

1 cup carrot juice

18 corn tortillas

2 cups cooked or canned pinto or black beans, drained and rinsed

Cover and bake for 30 minutes. Uncover and bake for 5 minutes longer. Cool for at least 15 minutes before cutting and serving.

Per serving: calories: 325, protein: 10 g, fat: 7 g, carbohydrate: 50 g, fiber: 12 g, sodium: 751 mg

Extra-Hearty Enchilada Casserole: Add 2 cups of chopped seitan to the onion sauce before assembling the casserole.

Seitan in Mexican Gravy

See photo facing page 144

MAKES 6 SERVINGS

I can almost hear the music playing in the busy market square of sunny Coyoacán, Mexico, when I make this dish. The art, history, and warmth of the Mexican people seem to permeate this recipe. Serve it over a bed of long-grain brown rice, with a fresh green salad on the side.

2 tablespoons water

1 teaspoon sesame oil

½ cup diced cabbage

½ cup diced carrot

½ cup diced onion

2 cloves garlic, minced (2 teaspoons)

1 teaspoon ground cumin

Sea salt

4 cups sliced or cubed seitan

2 cups vegetable broth

1 cup organic masa or corn flour, mixed with 1 cup cold water

1 tablespoon wheat-free tamari

¼ cup chopped fresh cilantro, for garnish

Heat the water and oil in a medium saucepan over medium heat. Add the cabbage, carrot, onion, garlic, cumin, and a pinch of salt. Cook and stir for 5 minutes, or until the vegetables are tender. Add a splash of water, if needed, to prevent sticking. Add the seitan, broth, and masa mixture. Bring to a gentle boil over medium-high heat, stirring constantly. Decrease the heat to low, cover, and cook for 30 minutes. If the mixture becomes too thick, add a little water to thin the gravy.

Add the tamari and cook for 5 minutes longer. Serve hot, garnished with the cilantro.

Per serving: calories: 426, protein: 50 g, fat: 3 g, carbohydrate: 39 g, fiber: 8 g, sodium: 186 mg

vegetables

Delectable Vegetables

IT'S AMAZING WHAT VEGETABLES CAN DO FOR US. We've all heard that eating brightly colored fruits and vegetables is good for us. That's because the rainbow of colorful vegetables is rich in a broad array of vitamins and antioxidants, which keep our cells healthy and immune systems strong, protecting our bodies from free radical damage and helping to prevent disease. Take a look at your plate and begin to notice what colors you're eating. When you use a colorful palette of ingredients, your meals can be a beautiful feast for the eyes as well as the body!

Besides focusing on getting lots of color onto your plate, also consider the way vegetables grow. The three categories I emphasize in cooking are roots, rounds, and leafy greens. Root vegetables are those that grow deep into the ground, such as burdock root, carrots, daikon, and parsnips. Round vegetables grow close to the ground, and these include brussels sprouts, cabbage, cauliflower, onions, rutabagas, and squash. Leafy greens, like bok choy, collard greens, and kale, reach for the sun with graceful determination.

There's a long-held theory that the growth patterns and energetic qualities of the vegetables we consume influence how we feel. According to the theory, root vegetables can help us feel grounded and strong. Round, or ground, vegetables can help us feel calm and relaxed. Leafy green vegetables might make us feel more flexible, energized, and able to reach for our goals. But don't just take my word for all of this: experiment with these various foods and see how they make you feel.

I divide vegetable-cooking methods into two basic categories: light cooking and long cooking. Light-cooking styles include blanching, sautéing, steaming, and stir-frying. Long-cooking styles include baking, pressure cooking, and stewing.

It would be hard to eat too many vegetables. This is one food group you can indulge in as much as you want! Veggies are low in calories and fat and high in vitamins, minerals, fiber, and all the good stuff. Use the following recipes to begin your love affair with veggies.

Steamed Greens `GLUTEN FREE`

MAKES 4 SERVINGS

Dark green leafy vegetables are superfoods and calcium champs. This is a food-in-a-flash recipe—it's not only quick, it's also easy.

10 cups washed and sliced dark green leafy vegetables (such as bok choy, collard greens, kale, and/or mustard greens)

Place a stainless steel steamer basket in a large pot with enough water to cover the bottom of the pot. Put the vegetables in the steamer, cover the pot, and bring to a boil over high heat. Steam for 2 to 3 minutes, or until the vegetables are tender. Transfer to a serving bowl. Serve plain or with your favorite dressing.

Per serving: calories: 85, protein: 6 g, fat: 1 g, carbohydrate: 14 g, fiber: 3 g, sodium: 73 mg

Stir-Fried Asian Greens GLUTEN FREE

MAKES 4 SERVINGS

Toasted sesame oil adds a distinctly Asian flavor to this tasty greens dish. Don't worry if it looks like a huge bush of greens that barely fits in your pot. It will shrink down substantially!

2 tablespoons water

6 cups thinly sliced bok choy

4 cups stemmed and torn kale
(in bite-sized pieces)

2 tablespoons mirin

1 teaspoon wheat-free tamari

¼ cup currants

1 teaspoon toasted sesame oil

¼ cup pine nuts, for garnish

Heat the water in a large skillet or wok over medium-high heat. Add the bok choy, kale, and a few drops of the mirin and tamari. Stir lightly. Cover and steam until the greens are wilted, 1 to 2 minutes.

Add the remaining mirin and tamari along with the currants. Cook and stir for 3 minutes longer, just until the greens are tender. Remove from the heat, add the oil, and stir lightly. Serve hot, garnished with the pine nuts.

Per serving: calories: 160, protein: 6 g, fat: 8 g, carbohydrate: 17 g, fiber: 4 g, sodium: 246 mg

Blanched Vegetables `GLUTEN FREE`

MAKES 4 SERVINGS

Light, colorful, and refreshing, blanched, or parboiled, vegetables are one of my staples. When you make big batches of blanched veggies, you'll have delicious, healthful snacks for munching on all day long. Serve them with a sprinkle of brown rice vinegar or your favorite dressing or dip.

4 leaves napa cabbage

Pinch sea salt

1 cup broccoli florets

1 cup cauliflower florets

1 carrot, cut into long, thick matchsticks

Slice the cabbage diagonally into 1-inch pieces. Put several inches of water in a medium pot and bring to a boil over high heat. Add the salt. Drop the cabbage into the water and let it remain there for less than 1 minute. Remove the cabbage with a slotted spoon or fine-mesh skimmer and transfer to a colander in the sink to drain and cool. Repeat this process with the broccoli, cauliflower, and carrot. (The idea is to cook the mildest and most lightly colored vegetables first, so that each vegetable retains its distinctive taste and hue.)

Per serving: calories: 26, protein: 2 g, fat: 0 g, carbohydrate: 4 g, fiber: 2 g, sodium: 77 mg

Variations: Use a mix of at least two different types of vegetables. Here are some additional combinations:

• bok choy, cabbage (red or green cabbage), watercress

• brussels sprouts, mustard greens, yellow summer squash

• carrots, collard greens, red radishes

• daikon, lacinato kale, red onion

Bok Choy Stir-Fry GLUTEN FREE

MAKES 6 SERVINGS

If you're new to eating leafy green vegetables, bok choy is a gentle introduction. Mild-tasting and crunchy, it's the perfect choice for steaming and stir-frying.

2 tablespoons vegetable broth

1 teaspoon sesame oil

1 cup carrot matchsticks

1 teaspoon peeled and minced fresh ginger

5 cups thinly sliced bok choy

1 cup broccoli florets

1 cup sliced napa cabbage

1 cup thinly sliced red cabbage

2 tablespoons mirin

1 teaspoon wheat-free tamari

1 tablespoon toasted black or tan sesame seeds

Heat the broth and oil in a large skillet or wok over medium-high heat. Add the carrot and ginger and cook and stir for 2 minutes. Add the bok choy, broccoli, napa cabbage, red cabbage, mirin, and tamari. Add a little more broth, if needed, to prevent the vegetables from sticking to the skillet. Cover and steam for about 5 minutes, or until bright and crisp-tender. Drain any excess liquid. Transfer to a serving dish and sprinkle with the sesame seeds. Serve hot.

Per serving: calories: 53, protein: 2 g, fat: 2 g, carbohydrate: 6 g, fiber: 2 g, sodium: 150 mg

Green Beans Amandine GLUTEN FREE

A culinary classic, this simple combination of green beans and almonds is always a hit.

4 cups trimmed green beans

½ cup water

¼ teaspoon sea salt,
   plus more as needed

½ cup slivered almonds

1 teaspoon extra-virgin olive oil

Ground black pepper

Put the green beans, water, and salt in a medium sauce pan over medium-high heat. Cover and cook for 5 minutes, or until tender to your liking.

Drain the beans and transfer to a bowl. Add the almonds and oil and toss until evenly distributed. Season with additional salt and pepper to taste and toss again gently. Serve hot.

Per serving: calories: 139, protein: 5 g, fat: 9 g, carbohydrate: 8 g, fiber: 6 g, sodium: 142 mg

Peppered Greens GLUTEN FREE

The color contrast in this dish—just a hint of crimson peeking out among the calcium-rich greens—is irresistible.

½ cup vegetable broth or water

1 red onion, cut in half and thinly sliced into half-moons

1 clove garlic, minced (1 teaspoon)

½ cup diced red bell pepper

6 leaves collard greens, stemmed, cut in half lengthwise, and sliced into thin ribbons (about 5 cups)

5 cups stemmed and torn kale (torn into bite-sized pieces)

¼ teaspoon sea salt

Heat 2 tablespoons of the broth in a large skillet over medium-high heat. Add the onion and garlic and cook and stir for 5 minutes, or until the onion is translucent. Add a little extra water if the onion begins to stick to the skillet. Add the bell pepper and cook and stir for 3 minutes. Add the collard greens, kale, salt, and remaining broth. Stir lightly and quickly. Cover and steam for 3 minutes. Remove the cover and toss lightly. Cook a little longer, if needed, just until the greens are tender. Serve plain or with your favorite dressing.

Per serving: calories: 82, protein: 5 g, fat: 1 g, carbohydrate: 12 g, fiber: 5 g, sodium: 192 mg

Beet Salad

You just can't beat this salad (and I can't resist a pun). This light, lemony salad will seduce even the most ardent beet antagonists into surrendering their positions.

4 beets, sliced into
   ¼-inch-thick rounds

½ cup finely diced red onion

1 tablespoon umeboshi vinegar

1 cup grated carrot

2 tablespoons gluten-free
   brown rice syrup

1 tablespoon extra-virgin
   olive oil

1 tablespoon brown rice
   vinegar or freshly squeezed
   lemon juice

Pinch sea salt

½ cup minced fresh dill

Steam the beets in a steamer basket over boiling water for 15 minutes, or until tender. Transfer to a large bowl to cool.

While the beets are steaming, put the onion and umeboshi vinegar in a small bowl. Mix well with your fingers, rubbing the vinegar into the onion. Marinate at room temperature for 10 minutes.

Add the carrot and onion to the beets.

Combine the syrup, oil, brown rice vinegar, and salt in a small bowl. Whisk until well blended. Pour over the vegetables. Add the dill and gently stir to combine. Cover and refrigerate until thoroughly chilled before serving.

Per serving: calories: 118, protein: 2 g, fat: 4 g, carbohydrate: 16 g, fiber: 4 g, sodium: 873 mg

Snap Pea Medley

MAKES 4 SERVINGS

For this snappy dish, the vegetables should be tender but still retain their crispness and bright color.

2 tablespoons water

2 cloves garlic, minced (2 teaspoons)

2 cups button mushrooms, cleaned and sliced

Sea salt

2 cups trimmed snap peas

1 small yellow summer squash, cut in half lengthwise and sliced thinly on a diagonal

½ cup carrot matchsticks

½ cup mung bean sprouts

Mirin, as needed

Heat the water in a large skillet over medium-high heat. Add the garlic and cook and stir for 30 seconds. Add the mushrooms and a pinch of salt. Cook and stir for 3 minutes. Cover and steam for 3 minutes longer, or until the mushrooms soften.

Add the snap peas, squash, carrot, and bean sprouts and lightly stir. Add a splash of mirin to prevent the vegetables from sticking to the skillet. Season with a little more salt to taste. Cook and stir just until the snap peas are bright and crisp-tender. Serve hot.

Per serving: calories: 56, protein: 4 g, fat: 0 g, carbohydrate: 7 g, fiber: 3 g, sodium: 11 mg

Seitan in Mexican Gravy, page 136

Sensuous Poached Pears, page 165

Baked Onions `GLUTEN FREE`

S weet, glossy, and oh so delicious. Pop these babies in the oven and prepare for a yummy treat.

4 medium onions, peeled

½ cup mirin

1 tablespoon sweet white miso, mixed with 3 tablespoons water

2 tablespoons balsamic vinegar

1 tablespoon wheat-free tamari, or a few pinches sea salt

1 teaspoon dried basil

½ teaspoon dried thyme

¼ teaspoon dried oregano

2 teaspoons kuzu starch, mixed with 2 tablespoons water

1 tablespoon minced fresh parsley, for garnish

Preheat the oven to 350 degrees F. Lightly oil a 7 x 11-inch glass baking dish.

Slice each onion vertically into 4 pieces and put them in the prepared baking dish.

Combine the mirin, diluted miso, vinegar, tamari, basil, thyme, and oregano in a small bowl and whisk until well blended. Spoon evenly over the onions. Cover with foil and bake for 1 hour, or until the onions are soft and caramelized.

Using a slotted spoon, transfer the onions to a serving bowl. Pour the remaining juices into a small saucepan. Add the kuzu mixture and stir gently over medium heat until thick and shiny. If the mixture becomes too thick, add a little extra mirin or water. Pour over the onions. Serve hot, garnished with the parsley.

Per serving: calories: 139, protein: 3 g, fat: 0 g, carbohydrate: 30 g, fiber: 3 g, sodium: 601 mg

Steamed Sweet Potato Melt GLUTEN FREE

MAKES 4 SERVINGS

It still amazes me that naturally sweet vegetable dishes like this one can satisfy even a recovered sugar addict like me. Mochi, which is made from brown rice, resembles a hard parmesan cheese; it can be found in the refrigerated section of most natural-food stores.

1 (2-inch) piece kombu, soaked in water for 10 minutes and drained

4 medium sweet potatoes, peeled and cut into ½-inch rounds (about 6 cups)

1⅓ cups freshly squeezed orange juice, plus more as needed

½ teaspoon sea salt

¼ cup tahini

2 teaspoons dried dill weed

2 teaspoons freshly squeezed lemon juice

3 cups coarsely grated mochi

½ cup chopped fresh parsley, for garnish

Chop the kombu into very small pieces and scatter it in a large skillet. Arrange the sweet potato rounds on top of the kombu. Add 1 cup of the orange juice and bring to a boil over medium-high heat. Decrease the heat to low, cover, and cook for 20 minutes. Check occasionally to make sure the orange juice has not evaporated, and add a little more if needed. Sprinkle with ¼ teaspoon of the salt and cook for 5 to 10 minutes longer.

Combine the tahini, remaining ⅓ cup of orange juice, dill weed, lemon juice, and remaining ¼ teaspoon of salt in a small bowl and stir until well blended. Drizzle over the sweet potatoes. Top with the mochi, cover, and cook for 5 minutes, or until the liquid has evaporated and the mochi resembles melted cheese. Serve hot, garnished with the parsley.

Per serving: calories: 545, protein: 11 g, fat: 9 g, carbohydrate: 101 g, fiber: 9 g, sodium: 328 mg

Kinpira Root Vegetables GLUTEN FREE

This traditional Japanese root-vegetable dish is very fortifying. It's perfect for whenever you need an energy pick-me-up, or for people like me who are on their feet a lot. Although optional, the ginger juice adds a little warming zip to this dish.

1 teaspoon sesame oil

1 cup plus 2 tablespoons water, plus more as needed

3 cups burdock root matchsticks

3 cups carrot matchsticks

2 teaspoons wheat-free tamari

2 teaspoons peeled and grated fresh ginger (optional)

Lightly brush the bottom of a large skillet with the oil. Add 2 tablespoons of the water and put over medium-high heat. Add the burdock root and cook and stir for 3 minutes. Put the carrots on top of the burdock root without stirring.

Add the remaining cup of water and a few drops of the tamari. Cover and cook over medium-high heat for 20 minutes, or until the vegetables are tender. Check the water level occasionally to make sure it has not evaporated, and add a little more if needed.

Sprinkle the vegetables evenly with the remaining tamari, cover, and cook until the liquid evaporates. At the end of the cooking time, put the optional ginger in your hand and squeeze it over the vegetables to extract the juice. Serve hot.

Per serving: calories: 77, protein: 2 g, fat: 1 g, carbohydrate: 13 g, fiber: 3 g, sodium: 157 mg

Variations: Use a mix of at least two different types of vegetables. Here are some additional combinations:

• burdock root, carrot, and green beans

• burdock root, carrot, and thinly sliced fresh lotus root

• carrots, parsnips, and snap peas

• turnips and red onion

African Vegetable Stew `GLUTEN FREE`

MAKES 4 TO 6 SERVINGS

I love the taste of sweet spices in a savory dish. Serve this stew over brown rice couscous with a side of boiled collard greens.

1 (2-inch) piece kombu, soaked in water for 10 minutes and drained

2 bay leaves

3 cups diced sweet potatoes (in 1-inch cubes; peeling is optional)

2 carrots, sliced into 1/4-inch-thick rounds (about 2 cups)

2 cups sliced celery (in 1-inch pieces)

1/2 cup diced green cabbage (in 1-inch cubes)

3 cups vegetable broth, plus more as needed

1 cup cooked or canned chickpeas, drained and rinsed

1 cup bite-sized seitan chunks (optional)

1/3 cup raisins

Finely chop the kombu and put it in a large stewpot with the bay leaves. Add the sweet potatoes, carrots, celery, and cabbage. Add the broth and bring to a boil over medium-high heat. Decrease the heat to low, cover, and simmer until the vegetables are tender, about 25 minutes.

Add the chickpeas, optional seitan, raisins, tamari, vinegar, syrup, cinnamon, cloves, and turmeric. Cover and cook for 15 minutes, adding a little more broth, if needed, to achieve the desired consistency.

- 1 tablespoon wheat-free tamari

- 1 tablespoon umeboshi vinegar

- 1 tablespoon gluten-free brown rice syrup or maple syrup

- 1 teaspoon ground cinnamon

- 1/8 teaspoon ground cloves

- 1/8 teaspoon ground turmeric

- 1/3 cup chunky peanut butter, mixed with 1/3 cup warm water

- 2 cups bite-sized kale pieces

- 2 tablespoons kuzu or arrowroot starch, mixed with 1/4 cup water

- 1/8 teaspoon cayenne (optional)

- 1/3 cup shelled pistachios, for garnish

- 3 tablespoons lemon zest, for garnish

- 1/4 cup chopped fresh parsley, for garnish

Pour the peanut butter mixture over the vegetables. Add the kale, kuzu mixture, and optional cayenne. Simmer uncovered, stirring occasionally, for 5 minutes, until the sauce has thickened and the kale is tender. Serve hot, topped with the pistachios, lemon zest, and parsley.

Per serving: calories: 434, protein: 16 g, fat: 13 g, carbohydrate: 58 g, fiber: 12 g, sodium: 978 mg

Glazed Brussels Sprouts
and Chestnuts GLUTEN FREE

MAKES 6 SERVINGS

Don't wait for a holiday to enjoy this festive dish. Cruciferous vegetables, like brussels sprouts, are loaded with anticancer compounds.

4 cups fresh brussels sprouts, cleaned and cut in half

1 cup peeled, roasted chestnuts (see note) or canned chestnuts

⅓ cup gluten-free brown rice syrup or maple syrup

2 tablespoons freshly squeezed lemon juice

1 tablespoon grapeseed oil or other oil

1 teaspoon lemon zest

¼ teaspoon sea salt

⅛ teaspoon ground nutmeg

Ground black pepper (optional)

Preheat the oven to 350 degrees F.

Put a few inches of water in a medium saucepan. Add a pinch of salt and bring to a boil over medium-high heat. Drop the brussels sprouts into the boiling water and cook for 5 minutes, or until fork-tender but still bright in color. Using a slotted spoon, transfer to a colander in the sink and rinse under cold water. Transfer the brussels sprouts to an 8 x 11-inch glass baking dish. Add the chestnuts.

Combine the syrup, lemon juice, oil, lemon zest, salt, nutmeg, and optional pepper to taste in a small bowl. Whisk until well blended. Drizzle over the brussels sprouts and chestnuts and stir to coat. Cover the dish with foil and bake for 30 minutes. Uncover and bake for 10 minutes longer. Serve hot.

Note: To roast fresh chestnuts, preheat the oven to 425 degrees F. Clean the chestnuts with a damp towel. Score the chestnut shells on one side with a paring knife, making a small cross on each one. Spread the chestnuts on a baking sheet, cut-side up, and bake for 15 to 25 minutes. Cool completely, then peel.

Per serving: calories: 122, protein: 3 g, fat: 3 g, carbohydrate: 18 g, fiber: 4 g, sodium: 106 mg

Stewed Nishime Vegetables GLUTEN FREE

MAKES 4 SERVINGS

Nishime (pronounced nish-ih-may) is a Japanese term for waterless cooking. Although this cooking method does require water, it is very minimal, resulting in extremely sweet-tasting vegetables. Occasionally I add greens, such as daikon or turnip greens, at the end. In warm weather, you can make the dish lighter by cutting the vegetables more thinly and cooking them for ten to twenty minutes. In cold weather, create a more warming dish by using large chunks of vegetables and cooking them for thirty to forty minutes.

1 (2-inch) piece kombu, soaked in water for 10 minutes, drained, and sliced into small strips

2 cups large chunks cabbage

2 onions, each cut vertically into 4 pieces

1 cup sliced daikon root (in 1/2-inch-thick rounds)

1 carrot, thickly sliced on a diagonal

3/4 cup water

2 tablespoons sweet white miso, mixed with 2 tablespoons water

Put the kombu in a large pot. Layer the cabbage on top of the kombu, followed by a layer of the onion, a layer of the daikon, and a final layer of the carrot. Alternatively, put each of the vegetables in sections around the pot. Add the water, cover, and bring to a boil over medium-high heat. Decrease the heat to low and cook the vegetables, without stirring, for 20 minutes. Occasionally check the water level and add a little more, if needed, to keep the vegetables from cooking dry.

When the vegetables are soft, add the diluted miso, cover, and gently shake the pot to coat the vegetables. Simmer for 10 minutes longer, or until the liquid has evaporated. Remove from the heat and let rest for 5 minutes before serving. Serve hot, with any remaining sauce.

Note: Any remaining sauce can be thickened by adding 1 teaspoon of kuzu or 2 teaspoons of arrowroot starch that has been mixed with 2 teaspoons of water. Simmer on low heat for 5 minutes, or until the sauce has thickened.

Per serving: calories: 68 protein: 3 g, fat: 11 g, carbohydrate: 11 g, fiber: 3 g, sodium: 251 mg

Variations: Use a mix of at least three different types of vegetables (the kombu should be included with all of them). Here are some additional combinations:

• cabbage, dried shiitake mushrooms, turnip

• carrot, onion, parsnip

• daikon, lotus root, winter squash

Mom's Sweet Potato Casserole GLUTEN FREE

MAKES 6 SERVINGS

It was always a special treat when Mom made this casserole. It's great for holidays or anytime you want a sweet addition to a meal.

3 medium sweet potatoes (about 2 pounds)

Few pinches sea salt

⅔ cup drained crushed pineapple or applesauce

1 tablespoon gluten-free brown rice syrup or maple syrup

2 teaspoons grapeseed oil or other oil

2 teaspoons ground cinnamon

Put the sweet potatoes in a large pot with water to cover. Bring to a boil over medium-high heat and cook for 30 to 40 minutes, or until the sweet potatoes are fork-tender. Transfer to a plate to cool. When the sweet potatoes are cool enough to handle, peel them and mash the flesh with a fork. Season with salt to taste.

Preheat the oven to 350 degrees F. Oil a 1½-quart oval casserole.

Put half the sweet potatoes in the prepared casserole. Top with the pineapple, syrup, 1 teaspoon of the oil, and 1 teaspoon of the cinnamon. Top with the remaining sweet potatoes. Drizzle with the remaining teaspoon of oil and sprinkle with the remaining teaspoon of cinnamon. Cover and bake for 35 to 40 minutes. Serve hot.

Per serving: calories: 172, protein: 3 g, fat: 2 g, carbohydrate: 32 g, fiber: 5 g, sodium: 57 mg

Oven-Roasted Vegetables GLUTEN FREE

MAKES 6 SERVINGS

It doesn't get much cozier in the kitchen than when root vegetables are roasting in the oven. They're sweet as candy.

2 carrots, very thinly sliced
   on a diagonal

2 medium parsnips, peeled
   and very thinly sliced
   on a diagonal

2 stalks celery,
   cut into 1-inch pieces

1 cup peeled and cubed
   butternut squash

1 beet, sliced into wedges

1 sweet potato, cubed
   (do not peel)

1 apple, cored and cubed
   (do not peel)

⅓ cup mirin

2 tablespoons grapeseed oil
   or other oil

1½ tablespoons balsamic
   vinegar

1 teaspoon dried thyme

½ teaspoon sea salt

Ground black pepper

Preheat the oven to 400 degrees F.

Put the carrots, parsnips, celery, squash, beet, sweet potato, and apple on a baking sheet with a ½-inch rim, or put them in a baking dish large enough to hold them in a single layer. Evenly sprinkle with the mirin, oil, vinegar, thyme, salt, and pepper to taste. Cover with foil and bake for 30 minutes. Carefully turn the vegetables over, cover with the foil again, and bake for 30 minutes longer, or until the vegetables are soft. For a crispy exterior, remove the foil during the last 10 minutes of baking. Serve hot or warm.

Per serving: calories: 164, protein: 2 g, fat: 5 g, carbohydrate: 25 g, fiber: 5 g, sodium: 337 mg

Sesame Veggies GLUTEN FREE

MAKES 4 SERVINGS

Parsnips look like white carrots, but they have a stronger flavor than their orange cousins. They are a rich source of fiber and potassium. I rarely peel organic produce because many vitamins lie in the surface of the skin; but I do recommend peeling parsnips, since sometimes the skin can be bitter.

½ cup water

4 cups thick carrot matchsticks

4 parsnips, peeled and cut into thick matchsticks

8 napa cabbage leaves, cut crosswise into ¼-inch-thick slices

1 tablespoon sweet white miso, mixed with ¼ cup water

1 tablespoon brown rice vinegar

⅓ cup sesame seeds, toasted

¼ cup minced chives

Heat 2 tablespoons of the water in a large skillet or wok over medium-high heat. Add the carrots and cook and stir for 5 minutes. Put the parsnips on top of the carrots, add ½ cup of the water, and bring to a boil. Decrease the heat to low, cover, and simmer for 10 minutes. Add the cabbage, diluted miso, and vinegar. Cover and cook for 10 minutes longer. Sprinkle with the sesame seeds and chives and stir gently to coat the vegetables. Serve warm.

Per serving: calories: 272 protein: 7 g, fat: 7 g, carbohydrate: 37 g, fiber: 13 g, sodium: 172 mg

Spaghetti à la Squash GLUTEN FREE

Move over pasta! Spaghetti squash is a nice change of pace. It's low in calories and is a good source of many nutrients and fiber (something most spaghetti products lack). And, of course, it's great fun to pull the cooked "spaghetti" strands from the skin.

1 spaghetti squash,
  cut in half lengthwise

1 cup water

2 teaspoons dried basil

2 teaspoons minced garlic

1 teaspoon dried oregano

1 cup tomato sauce or
  Carrot-Beet Marinara Sauce
  (page 80)

4 cups coarsely grated mochi

3 tablespoons sweet white
  miso, mixed with ¼ cup
  warm water

¼ cup minced fresh parsley,
  for garnish

Preheat the oven to 350 degrees F. Lightly oil a 9 x 12-inch glass baking dish.

Put the squash cut-side down in the prepared baking dish. Add the water, cover with foil, and bake for 45 minutes, or until the squash is fork-tender. (Alternatively, steam the squash in a large steamer basket over boiling water for 20 minutes, or until fork-tender.)

Carefully turn the squash over and fluff the flesh with a fork to loosen the "spaghetti" strands. Sprinkle both halves evenly with the basil, garlic, and oregano. Top with the tomato sauce and sprinkle with the mochi. Spoon the diluted miso over the mochi. Cover with foil and bake for 15 minutes longer, or until the mochi has completely melted. Serve hot, garnished with the parsley.

Per serving: calories: 137, protein: 4 g, fat: 2 g, carbohydrate: 26 g, fiber: 3 g, sodium: 358 mg

Easy One-Skillet Meal `GLUTEN FREE`

This recipe is a good source of iron because it is prepared in a cast iron skillet. Food cooked in cast iron absorbs some of the iron directly from the cookware. But don't worry if you don't have a cast iron skillet; this recipe can also be prepared in a stainless steel skillet.

1 (2-inch) piece kombu, soaked in water for 10 minutes, drained, and sliced

4 ounces whole-grain or gluten-free noodles of your choice, cooked in boiling water until al dente and drained

3 dried shiitake mushrooms, soaked in 1 cup water for 30 minutes, or until soft, and drained

1 cup sliced onion (in half-moons)

1 cup finely sliced cabbage

1 cup thinly sliced carrot

1 cup cauliflower florets

1 cup sliced leek

1 cup firm tofu cubes

1 tablespoon wheat-free tamari

1 cup thinly sliced bok choy

Put the kombu on the bottom of a large cast iron skillet. Add the noodles, mushrooms, onion, cabbage, carrot, cauliflower, leek, and tofu in separate sections around the skillet. Add just enough water to cover the bottom of the skillet, along with a few drops of the tamari. Cover and cook over medium-high heat for 5 minutes. Add the bok choy and the remaining tamari. Cover and cook for 2 minutes longer. Serve hot.

Per serving: calories: 155 protein: 9 g, fat: 3 g, carbohydrate: 20 g, fiber: 5 g, sodium: 293 mg

Ruby Rutabagas   GLUTEN FREE

MAKES 4 SERVINGS

The rutabaga is said to be a hybrid cross between a turnip and cabbage. This cruciferous vegetable is a good source of vitamins A and C.

1 (1-inch) piece kombu, soaked in water for 10 minutes, drained, and finely chopped

4 small rutabagas, peeled and sliced into thin wedges

3 medium beets, sliced into thin rounds

1 red onion, sliced horizontally into 1/2-inch-thick rings

1/2 cup water

Pinch sea salt

2 stalks celery, sliced diagonally

1 tablespoon sweet white miso, mixed with 2 tablespoons water

2 teaspoons umeboshi vinegar

2 tablespoons minced fresh parsley, for garnish

Put the kombu in a large saucepan. Add the rutabagas, beets, and onion. Add the water and salt. Cover and bring to a gentle boil over medium-high heat. Decrease the heat to medium-low and simmer for 20 minutes.

Add the celery, diluted miso, and vinegar. Lightly shake the saucepan. Cook for 10 minutes longer, or until the liquid evaporates. Serve hot, garnished with the parsley.

Per serving: calories: 137, protein: 5 g, fat: 1 g, carbohydrate: 23 g, fiber: 7 g, sodium: 763 mg

THE NATURAL VEGAN KITCHEN   157

Breaded Cauliflower

Roasting makes everything taste great, and cauliflower is no exception. This recipe brings out cauliflower's rich, melt-in-your-mouth flavor.

6 cups cauliflower florets

¼ cup grapeseed oil or other oil

½ cup breadcrumbs

1 teaspoon dried Italian seasoning

½ teaspoon sea salt

Ground black pepper

¼ cup chopped fresh parsley, for garnish

Preheat the oven to 350 degrees F.

Steam the cauliflower in a steamer basket over boiling water for 5 minutes. Drain and transfer the cauliflower to a 9 x 12-inch glass baking dish. Drizzle evenly with 2 tablespoons of the oil. Evenly sprinkle the breadcrumbs, Italian seasoning, salt, and pepper to taste over the top. Drizzle evenly with the remaining 2 tablespoons of oil. Bake for 20 minutes, or until the cauliflower is golden and fork-tender. Serve hot, garnished with the parsley.

Per serving: calories: 216, protein: 5 g, fat: 15 g, carbohydrate: 13g, fiber: 4 g, sodium: 412 mg

Sweet-and-Sour Cabbage `GLUTEN FREE`

This dish makes a striking presentation, especially when served on a plate next to polenta and bok choy. The color is gorgeous and the flavor divine.

**2 Granny Smith apples,
peeled, cored, and sliced**

**1 red onion, sliced into
half-moons**

**4 cups shredded
red cabbage**

**½ cup unsweetened
apple juice**

Pinch sea salt

**⅓ cup gluten-free
brown rice syrup**

**1 tablespoon
brown rice vinegar**

**2 teaspoons
umeboshi vinegar**

Put the apples and onion in a medium pot. Put the cabbage on top. Add the apple juice and salt and bring to a gentle boil over medium-high heat. Decrease the heat to medium-low, cover, and cook for 30 minutes, or until the liquid has nearly evaporated.

Add the syrup, brown rice vinegar, and umeboshi vinegar. Cover and cook until the liquid has reduced and mostly evaporated, with very little remaining in the pot. If necessary, remove the cover and increase the heat to reduce the liquid more quickly. Serve warm or chilled.

Per serving: calories: 137, protein: 0 g, fat: 0 g, carbohydrate: 30 g, fiber: 3 g, sodium: 550 mg

222

CHAPTER ELEVEN

Have Your Cake and Eat It Too!

desserts

A WISE TEACHER GAVE ME GREAT ADVICE when I was first learning to cook with natural foods: He told me to become proficient at making desserts. I had confided in our counseling session that I had a wild sweet tooth and wanted to stop eating white sugar. His method proved genius—it worked! Having wholesome alternatives on hand kept me from diving into the strong stuff (most of the time), and gradually my cravings went from a lion's roar down to a mild meow.

Taste buds change. I used to have dessert three times a day. Now my palate has become sensitive enough that apple slices taste divinely sweet, and I say this as someone who used to consider carrot cake as one of the four food groups. The sweet taste of natural foods keeps me satisfied; if I got myself off sugar, I know that anyone can. On special occasions, or even a few times a week, use the following recipes for a healthful, delicious indulgence.

Apricot Mousse `GLUTEN FREE`

MAKES 4 SERVINGS

Apricots are rich in vitamin A and are a good source of vitamins C and E and potassium. Enjoy this gorgeous, creamy mousse garnished with fresh mint leaves.

1½ cups unsweetened apple juice

1½ cups original amazake or plain nondairy milk

1 cup dried apricots

¼ cup agar flakes

Pinch sea salt

2 teaspoons kuzu starch, mixed with 2 tablespoons cold water

¼ cup gluten-free brown rice syrup

1 tablespoon almond butter

1 teaspoon gluten-free vanilla extract

2 fresh apricots, sliced, for garnish

⅓ cup sliced almonds, for garnish

4 fresh mint leaves, for garnish

Put the juice, amazake, dried apricots, and agar flakes in a medium saucepan. Let the apricots soak in the liquid for 30 minutes.

Add the salt to the apricot mixture and bring to a boil over medium-high heat. Decrease the heat to low, cover, and simmer for 10 minutes.

Stir the kuzu mixture into the saucepan and continue stirring until the liquid thickens. Add the syrup and almond butter and simmer for 5 minutes longer. Remove from the heat and stir in the vanilla extract.

Pour the mixture into a blender and process until smooth. Pour into 4 parfait glasses and refrigerate for 3 hours, or until thoroughly chilled. Garnish with the fresh apricots, almonds, and mint leaves just before serving.

Per serving: calories: 325, protein: 5 g, fat: 7 g, carbohydrate: 59 g, fiber: 7 g, sodium: 35 mg

Cinnamon-Scented Poached Fruit `GLUTEN FREE`

According to macrobiotic theory, cooked fruit is less cooling to the digestive system, making it more digestible. Adding a touch of sea salt enhances the natural sweetness of fruit.

5 apples, peeled and sliced

½ cup gluten-free brown rice syrup

¼ cup unsweetened apple juice

Pinch sea salt

1 cup fresh or frozen red raspberries

1 cup fresh or frozen blueberries

1 tablespoon kuzu starch, mixed with 2 tablespoons cold water

1 teaspoon gluten-free vanilla extract

Few dashes ground cinnamon, plus more for garnish

Soy whipped cream, for garnish

6 fresh mint leaves, for garnish

Combine the apples, syrup, juice, and salt in a medium saucepan and bring to a gentle boil over medium heat. Decrease the heat to low, cover, and simmer for 10 minutes.

Add the raspberries, blueberries, kuzu mixture, vanilla extract, and cinnamon. Stir gently until the mixture becomes glossy and thick. Add a little more juice if it becomes too thick. Serve warm, garnished with soy whipped cream, a mint leaf, and a sprinkle of cinnamon.

Per serving: calories: 142, protein: 1 g, fat: 1 g, carbohydrate: 32 g, fiber: 4 g, sodium: 4 mg

Lemon Kanten Parfait `GLUTEN FREE`

MAKES 8 PARFAITS

This dessert has it all: layers of refreshing apple kanten, rich cashew cream, and crunchy cookie crumbs. Garnish it with a mint leaf and you've got a lovely parfait.

Lemon Kanten

2 cups unsweetened apple juice

1 tablespoon agar flakes, soaked in 2 tablespoons water for 30 minutes

¼ cup freshly squeezed lemon juice

2 tablespoons gluten-free brown rice syrup or maple syrup

Pinch sea salt

2 tablespoons kuzu starch, mixed with ¼ cup cold water

Cashew Cream

2 cups raw cashews

1 cup cold water

½ cup maple syrup

1 teaspoon gluten-free vanilla extract

⅛ teaspoon almond extract

Pinch sea salt

Layers and Garnish

2 cups crushed cookies, granola, or toasted nuts

4 lemon slices, for garnish

4 fresh mint leaves, for garnish

To make the kanten, put the apple juice and agar mixture in a saucepan. Whisk in the lemon juice, syrup, and salt and bring to a boil over medium-high heat. Decrease the heat to low, cover, and cook for 10 minutes. Add the kuzu mixture and stir until thickened. Remove from the heat and pour into a metal bowl to cool, whisking periodically. When the kanten is room temperature, put it in the refrigerator, uncovered, to chill for 2 hours, whisking occasionally.

To make the cashew cream, combine the cashews, water, syrup, vanilla extract, almond extract, and salt in a blender or food processor. Process until smooth.

To assemble, layer the kanten, cashew cream, and cookies in 4 parfait glasses, ending with a dollop of the cashew cream. Cover and chill for 1 hour before serving. Just before serving, garnish with the lemon slices and mint leaves.

Per parfait: calories: 437, protein: 10 g, fat: 22 g, carbohydrate: 51 g, fiber: 4 g, sodium: 15 mg

Sensuous Poached Pears `GLUTEN FREE`

See photo facing page 145

MAKES 4 SERVINGS

I can think of nothing sexier than poached pears for dessert. The cranberry juice stains them a sultry shade of crimson.

4 whole Bosc pears, peeled, with the stems intact

½ cup unsweetened apple-cranberry juice

½ cup gluten-free brown rice syrup or maple syrup

½ cup red wine or additional apple-cranberry juice

2 cinnamon sticks, or 1½ teaspoons ground cinnamon

1 teaspoon whole cloves, or ¼ teaspoon ground cloves

Pinch sea salt

1 tablespoon arrowroot starch, mixed with ¼ cup cold water

2 teaspoons lemon zest, for garnish

Ground cinnamon, for garnish

Slice a very thin piece from the bottom of each pear. Arrange the pears standing upright in a large pot.

Combine the juice, syrup, wine, cinnamon sticks, cloves, and salt in a small bowl. Pour over the pears and bring to a gentle boil over medium heat. Decrease the heat to medium-low, cover, and simmer for 30 minutes, or until the pears are tender. Occasionally spoon the sauce over the pears while they are cooking. Alternatively, bake the pears uncovered at 400 degrees F for 1 hour, occasionally spooning the sauce over them.

Transfer the pears to serving plates. Using a slotted spoon, remove the solid spices from the cooking liquid. (If the liquid has completely evaporated, add ¼ cup juice, ¼ cup gluten-free brown rice syrup, and ¼ cup red wine to the pot.) Add the arrowroot mixture to the cooking liquid and stir over low heat until thickened. Adjust the consistency, if needed. To thin, add more liquid. To thicken, add a little more diluted arrowroot and simmer for a few more minutes.

To serve, drizzle the pears with the sauce. Alternatively, spoon the syrup onto plates and put the pears on top. Sprinkle with the lemon zest. Decorate the edges of the plates with a dusting of cinnamon.

Per serving: calories: 228, protein: 1 g, fat: 1 g, carbohydrate: 47 g, fiber: 4 g, sodium: 7 mg

Orange-Kissed Fruits `GLUTEN FREE`

Simple and delicious. I love uncomplicated recipes!

2 Golden Delicious apples, cut into large chunks

2 ripe Bartlett pears, cut into large chunks

½ cup orange or tangerine sections, seeds removed

⅓ cup freshly squeezed orange juice

¼ cup gluten-free brown rice syrup

1 tablespoon orange zest

Pinch sea salt

2 teaspoons kuzu starch, mixed with 2 tablespoons cold water

Put the apples, pears, orange sections, juice, syrup, zest, and salt in a saucepan and bring to a boil over medium-high heat. Decrease the heat to medium-low and simmer for 10 minutes. Add the kuzu mixture and stir gently until a shiny glaze forms. Serve warm.

Per serving: calories: 155, protein: 1 g, fat: 1 g, carbohydrate: 34 g, fiber: 5 g, sodium: 3 mg

Jelled Fruit Dessert GLUTEN FREE

This light dessert uses a sea vegetable called agar to help it jell, rather than conventional gelatin, which is made from animal products.

3 cups unsweetened apple juice

1 cup fresh fruit, such as berries, sliced apple or pear, or melon balls

4 tablespoons agar flakes

Pinch sea salt

Put the juice, fruit (see note), agar flakes, and salt in a medium saucepan and bring to a gentle boil over medium-high heat. Decrease the heat to low and simmer for 10 minutes, until the agar flakes have completely dissolved.

Pour into 4 individual dessert cups or fun-shaped molds. Cool, uncovered, in the refrigerator for about 2 hours, or until firm to the touch. Serve thoroughly chilled.

Note: If you are using hard fruits, such as apples or pears, add them at the beginning of the cooking process. If you are using soft fruits, such as berries, add them after the agar flakes have dissolved, at the very the end of the cooking time.

Per serving: calories: 129, protein: 1 g, fat: 0 g, carbohydrate: 29 g, fiber: 2 g, sodium: 13 mg

No-Bake Berry Pie
with Amazake Cream GLUTEN FREE

How cool is this—a pie you don't need to bake!

Pie Shell

½ cup millet

1¾ cups water or unsweetened apple juice

Pinch sea salt

¼ cup finely chopped toasted pecans

Berry Filling

1 cup unsweetened apple juice

3 tablespoons agar flakes

Pinch sea salt

2 tablespoons kuzu starch, mixed with 2 tablespoons cold water

2 cups fresh berries (blackberries, raspberries, strawberries, or a mixture)

1 cup Amazake Cream Topping (page 169)

Fresh mint leaves, for garnish

To make the pie shell, put the millet, water, and salt in a medium saucepan and bring to a boil. Decrease the heat to low, cover, and simmer for 25 minutes, or until the millet is soft. Add the pecans and mix well. Spoon into a 9-inch glass pie plate that has been rinsed with water but not dried. Spread the millet evenly using the back of a moistened spoon. Let cool.

To make the filling, combine the juice, agar flakes, and salt in a medium saucepan and bring to a boil over medium-high heat. Decrease the heat to low, cover, and cook for 15 minutes. Add the kuzu mixture and cook, stirring occasionally, until the mixture thickens, about 5 minutes. Fold in the berries and gently stir to coat them evenly. Remove from the heat.

Pour the berry mixture into the pie shell and refrigerate for 1 hour to cool. Serve thoroughly chilled, in slices, garnished with the Amazake Cream Topping and mint leaves.

Per serving: calories: 141, protein: 3 g, fat: 3 g, carbohydrate: 22 g, fiber: 4 g, sodium: 11 mg

Amazake Cream Topping GLUTEN FREE

MAKES 1 CUP

This low-fat topping will set off your desserts with just the right touch.

1 cup amazake (original, almond, or hazelnut)

1 tablespoon gluten-free brown rice syrup

1 tablespoon agar flakes

1 teaspoon gluten-free vanilla extract

Combine the amazake, syrup, and agar flakes in a small saucepan. Let soak for 10 minutes.

Bring to a simmer (not a rolling boil) over medium-high heat. Decrease the heat to low, cover, and simmer for 15 minutes, or until the agar has dissolved. Remove from the heat and stir in the vanilla extract.

Pour into a small bowl to cool. Once the mixture is cool, cover and refrigerate it until firm. When the mixture is firm, transfer it to a blender or food processor and process until smooth, adding extra amazake, if needed, to achieve a creamy consistency. Stored in a covered container in the refrigerator, Amazake Cream Topping will keep for 5 days.

Per ¼ cup: calories: 54, protein: 1 g, fat: 0 g, carbohydrate: 12 g, fiber: 0 g, sodium: 8 mg

Basmati Rice Pudding <small>GLUTEN FREE</small>

MAKES 4 SERVINGS

This pudding is a signature dessert in Indian cooking. I love the silky texture and faint aroma of roses.

2 cups cooked brown or white basmati rice

1 cup almond milk (vanilla or plain)

½ cup coconut milk

½ cup maple syrup, or ¼ cup maple syrup and ¼ cup gluten-free brown rice syrup

¼ cup currants

½ teaspoon ground cinnamon, plus more for garnish

Pinch ground cloves

Pinch ground nutmeg

1 teaspoon gluten-free vanilla extract

1 tablespoon rose water (optional)

½ cup slivered almonds or pistachio nuts

Combine the rice, almond milk, coconut milk, syrup, currants, cinnamon, cloves, and nutmeg in a medium saucepan and bring to a gentle boil over medium-high heat. Decrease the heat to low, cover, and simmer for 20 minutes, or until the desired consistency is achieved. (This pudding gets thicker the longer you cook it, and it will also thicken further as it cools.) Remove from the heat and stir in the vanilla extract and optional rose water.

Spoon into 4 dessert cups and sprinkle with cinnamon. Serve warm or chilled, garnished with the almonds.

Per serving: calories: 398, protein: 6 g, fat: 15 g, carbohydrate: 61 g, fiber: 4 g, sodium: 46 mg

Peachy Quinoa Pudding GLUTEN FREE

MAKES 4 SERVINGS

Quinoa's nutty taste lends itself nicely to this delicate, high-protein dessert.

2½ cups cooked quinoa (see note)

2 peaches, peeled and chopped

1 cup almond milk (vanilla or plain)

½ cup coconut milk

½ cup gluten-free brown rice syrup or maple syrup

2 teaspoons freshly squeezed lemon juice

1 teaspoon gluten-free vanilla extract

½ teaspoon ground cinnamon

Pinch sea salt

8 slices fresh peach, for garnish

½ cup fresh red raspberries, for garnish

4 fresh mint leaves, for garnish

Put the quinoa, chopped peaches, almond milk, coconut milk, syrup, lemon juice, vanilla extract, cinnamon, and salt in a medium saucepan and bring to a boil over medium-high heat. Decrease the heat to low and simmer for 15 minutes, or until the pudding is creamy.

Spoon into 4 parfait glasses. Serve warm or chilled, garnished with the peach slices, raspberries, and mint leaves.

Note: To cook the quinoa, bring 1½ cups of water to boil in a medium saucepan. Add ¾ cup of quinoa and a pinch of sea salt. Decrease the heat to low, cover, and cook for 20 minutes, or until the quinoa is fluffy and the water is absorbed.

Per serving: calories: 303, protein: 6 g, fat: 8 g, carbohydrate: 47 g, fiber: 4 g, sodium: 43 mg

Blueberry-Pear Fluff GLUTEN FREE

MAKES 4 SERVINGS

The pairing of pears with blueberries results in a refreshing, lightly sweet dessert with a gorgeous lavender color. Elegance and simplicity unite!

3 Bosc pears, peeled and diced

1 cup fresh blueberries

¼ cup gluten-free brown rice syrup

2 tablespoons unsweetened apple juice

¼ teaspoon ground cinnamon

Pinch sea salt

1 tablespoon kuzu starch, mixed with ¼ cup cold water

4 fresh mint leaves, for garnish

2 teaspoons lemon zest, for garnish

Combine the pears, blueberries, syrup, juice, cinnamon, and salt in a medium saucepan and bring to a gentle boil over medium-high heat. Decrease the heat to medium-low and simmer for 20 minutes, or until the pears are very soft. Add the kuzu mixture and stir gently until the mixture thickens. Transfer to a blender and process until smooth.

Spoon into 4 parfait glasses. Serve warm or chilled, garnished with the mint leaves and lemon zest.

Per serving: calories: 147, protein: 1 g, fat: 1 g, carbohydrate: 33 g, fiber: 4 g, sodium: 3 mg

Red Berry Mousse `GLUTEN FREE`

Berries are chock-full of antioxidants, making this beautiful red mousse a nutritious indulgence.

2 cups unsweetened apple juice

¼ cup agar flakes, soaked in ¼ cup cold water for 30 minutes

Pinch sea salt

1 cup sliced fresh strawberries

1 cup fresh red raspberries

¼ cup kuzu starch, mixed with ¼ cup cold water

1 teaspoon gluten-free vanilla extract

1 cup Amazake Cream Topping (page 169), for garnish

6 fresh red raspberries, for garnish

6 fresh mint leaves, for garnish

Combine the juice, agar mixture, and salt in a medium saucepan and bring to a boil over medium-high heat. Decrease the heat to low and simmer for 15 minutes. Add the strawberries, raspberries, and kuzu mixture, and stir until thickened. Remove from the heat and stir in the vanilla extract.

Pour into a blender or food processor and process until smooth. Transfer to a bowl, cover, and chill in the refrigerator until firm. Whisk well to create a fluffy texture, or process again in a blender or food processor, adding a little more apple juice if needed.

Spoon into 6 dessert cups. Garnish each serving with a dollop of Amazake Cream Topping, a raspberry, and a mint leaf.

Per serving: calories: 122, protein: 1 g, fat: 0 g, carbohydrate: 26 g, fiber: 4 g, sodium: 18 mg

Chocolate Pudding GLUTEN FREE

MAKES 8 SERVINGS

Sweet, rich, and chocolaty. Enjoy!

4 cups chocolate soymilk

½ cup maple syrup

¼ cup agar flakes, soaked in ½ cup cold water for 30 minutes

Pinch sea salt

¼ cup kuzu starch, mixed with ¼ cup cold water

½ cup nondairy chocolate chips

1 cup Tofu Whipped Cream, for garnish (page 176)

Put the soymilk, syrup, agar mixture, and salt in a medium saucepan. Bring to a boil over medium-high heat, stirring with a whisk periodically. Decrease the heat to low, cover, and simmer for 15 minutes. Add the kuzu mixture and chocolate chips and stir with a whisk until the mixture thickens and the chocolate chips have melted.

Pour into 4 dessert cups, cover, and refrigerate until thoroughly chilled. Serve cold, topped with the Tofu Whipped Cream.

Per serving: calories: 250, protein: 6 g, fat: 7 g, carbohydrate: 42 g, fiber: 2 g, sodium: 74 mg

Vanilla Amazake Custard GLUTEN FREE

Amazake is a creamy, sweet, fermented rice beverage that's as thick and creamy as a milkshake. This pudding is sweet enough on its own so that you don't need to add any sweetener. Serve the custard plain or topped with fresh fruit.

2 cups amazake (original, almond, or hazelnut)

2 teaspoons agar flakes

1 vanilla bean, or 1 teaspoon gluten-free vanilla extract

1 tablespoon kuzu starch, mixed with 2 tablespoon cold water

Put the amazake and agar flakes in a small saucepan and bring to a boil over medium-high heat, stirring constantly with a whisk. Decrease the heat to low, cover, and simmer for 20 minutes, or until the agar flakes are dissolved.

Slice the vanilla bean in half lengthwise and scrape the seeds into the amazake mixture. Add the kuzu mixture and stir until thickened. Pour into 4 dessert cups, cover, and refrigerate until firm. Serve thoroughly chilled.

Per serving: calories: 88, protein: 2 g, fat: 0 g, carbohydrate: 19 g, fiber: 0 g, sodium: 12 mg

THE NATURAL VEGAN KITCHEN 175

Tofu Whipped Cream GLUTEN FREE

MAKES 1½ CUPS

This dreamy whipped topping will add just the right touch to all of your desserts. It also goes great served with a bowl of fresh strawberries.

8 ounces firm tofu, drained and cubed

¼ cup maple syrup, plus more as needed

1 tablespoon cashew butter

1 teaspoon gluten-free vanilla extract

½ teaspoon almond extract

Combine all the ingredients in a food processor and process until smooth and creamy. Adjust the sweetness level to taste by adding a small amount of additional maple syrup.

Per ¼ cup: calories: 93, protein: 5 g, fat: 3 g, carbohydrate: 11 g, fiber: 1 g, sodium: 5 mg

Glossary

Adzuki beans. Adzuki beans are small, sweet-tasting red beans that are popular in traditional Japanese cooking.

Agar. Also known as kanten, agar is derived from refined sea vegetables and can replace gelatin in aspics and fruit gels.

Amazake. A creamy, sweet, thick beverage, amazake is made from fermented sweet brown rice that has been mixed with a starter called koji (see page 178).

Arame. A mild, slightly sweet, brownish-black sea vegetable, arame is most commonly available dried. Rehydrate it in water for use in vegetable sautés and salads.

Arrowroot. A fine white powder similar to cornstarch, arrowroot is used to thicken desserts, gravies, and sauces.

Barley malt. Barley malt is a thick sweetener made from malted barley. It has a flavor similar to molasses.

Black soybeans. Jet black cousins of yellow soybeans, black soybeans are sometimes difficult to find in natural food stores but can be ordered online (see Mail Order Suppliers, page 182).

Boiled salads and blanched vegetables. Boiled salads and blanched vegetables are made by briefly cooking vegetables in boiling water.

Couscous. Fast-cooking couscous is a granular semolina used to make desserts, pilafs, and salads. Gluten-free couscous made from roasted brown rice is also available.

Daikon. A long white radish, daikon can be grated or sliced and added to salads or served as a condiment with fried foods, like tempura. It can also be stewed or steamed.

Dulse. A coarse, dark red sea vegetable, dulse is often used in soups and condiments. When it is toasted, it has a smoky flavor reminiscent of bacon that makes it a welcome addition to salads and vegetarian BLT sandwiches.

Flame deflector. A flame deflector is a round metal disc with a handle. It is placed between the heating element and a pressure cooker or other cookware to distribute the heat more evenly and prevent ingredients from burning.

Gluten. Gluten, a protein found in certain grains, such as wheat, barley, rye, and spelt, gives structure to breads and baked goods. Wheat gluten is used to make seitan, also known as wheat meat.

Gomasio. Gomasio is a nutty-tasting condiment made from roasted sesame seeds and sea salt finely ground together.

Kanten. Kanten is a vegetarian jelled fruit dessert made from agar (see page 177) that is cooked into fruit juice and then chilled.

Kinpira. Kinpira is an Asian cooking style using root vegetables, such as burdock root and carrots, sliced into thin matchsticks, and then sautéed, simmered, and seasoned with tamari.

Koji. Koji is an enzyme preparation made from rice that is used to start the fermentation process of amazake, miso, sake, and tamari.

Kombu. A thick, dark-colored sea vegetable (kelp), kombu is used to tenderize beans and flavor broths, such as Japanese dashi. It is also used in condiments, stewed vegetables, and even candy.

Kuzu starch. Kuzu starch is made from the tuberous roots of the fast-growing kudzu plant. The kudzu root is dried and ground into a starchy powder, which is used as a thickener in soups and sauces. Kuzu starch is considered more wholesome and digestible than cornstarch.

Lotus root. The edible root of a water lily, lotus root has brown skin; long, hollow chambers; and off-white, crisp flesh. It is used as a vegetable in stir-fries and soups in Asian cooking. Avoid bright white store-bought lotus root, as it has been bleached to make it snowy white.

Masa. Made from whole corn that has been cooked in limewater and then ground into a dough, masa is traditionally used in Mexico and South America to make arepas (stuffed cornbread), tamales, and tortillas.

Millet. A small, round yellow grain, millet is a staple in Asia and Africa. It has a mild, sweet flavor that makes it ideal for use in soups and pilafs. Ground millet is used in breads, porridges, and puddings. When millet is cooked with cauliflower and mashed, it makes a nutritious alternative to whipped potatoes.

Mirin. Mirin is a sweet Japanese cooking wine made from glutinous rice (it does not contain gluten) and koji (see page 178). It is used as a seasoning in glazes and sauces.

Miso. A paste made from fermented soybeans or other legumes and grains, miso comes in many varieties that differ in color, flavor, and saltiness. Light-colored miso tends to be mild and sweet, whereas darker miso usually has been fermented longer and has a stronger, saltier flavor. Miso is used extensively in Asian cuisine to flavor salad dressings, sauces, soups, spreads, main dishes, and marinades. Because of the active enzymes and beneficial bacteria it contains, miso aids digestion.

Mochi. Mochi is made from sweet, sticky short-grain rice that has been cooked and then dried into blocks. It can be used to make chewy soup croutons or a quick pan-puffed snack and is sometimes used in desserts. It can also be grated and added to casseroles for a cheesy texture.

Nishime. Nishime is a braised Japanese vegetable dish made with kombu (see page 178) and tamari (see page 181). The vegetables are cooked slowly, on low heat, until all the liquid has evaporated, resulting in a very sweet taste.

Nori. A dried sea vegetable sold in paper-thin sheets, nori is wrapped around rice balls and sushi. It is also used as a condiment and seasoning.

Polenta. A creamy cereal or side dish made from cooked corn grits, polenta is a staple in northern Italian cooking. It can be served hot and creamy, or, if it has cooled until firm, it can be cut into pieces and fried.

Rice syrup. A thick sweetener similar to honey but far less sweet, rice syrup is made by culturing cooked rice with enzymes. Most rice syrups contain barley, a gluten-containing grain. If you need to avoid gluten, look for gluten-free rice syrup.

Sea salt. Sea salt is made by the evaporation of seawater. It is higher in trace minerals and slightly lower in sodium than commercial table salt and is free from additives.

Shiitake mushrooms. Native to Japan, shiitake mushrooms are popular in miso soup, cooked vegetable combinations, and simmered dishes. A medicinal mushroom, the shiitake is grown seasonally and is therefore most often available dried. Dried shiitake mushrooms must be reconstituted in water prior to using.

Sweet brown rice. Sweet brown rice is a glutinous rice that cooks up sticky and sweet. (It does not contain any gluten.) It is used to make amazake (see page 177), brown rice vinegar, and mochi (see page 179).

Tahini. Tahini is a spread similar to peanut butter but made from ground sesame seeds. It is used to make dips, dressings, sauces, and spreads.

Tamari. A wheat-free by-product of the miso-making process, tamari is used as a condiment and seasoning.

Tempeh. A traditional and popular food in Indonesia, Sri Lanka, and Southeast Asia, tempeh is made by inoculating split soybeans with a beneficial bacteria for several hours. Tempeh has a distinctive flavor and chewy texture compared with tofu. It is used as a protein source in casseroles, salads, stews, and stir fries.

Tofu. Also known as bean curd, tofu is made from curdled soymilk. Fresh tofu is mild-tasting and comes in textures that range from soft to extra-firm. It is versatile and can be used to make desserts, lasagne, salad dressings, scrambles, soups, and vegan quiches.

Umeboshi plum. Extremely salty and sour-flavored, Japanese umeboshi plums are made from a fruit that is closely related to the apricot. The immature fruit is pickled with sea salt and shiso (perilla) leaves. Ume plums, as they are often called, add a tangy, salty flavor to drinks, rice balls, sauces, snacks, and sushi.

Umeboshi plum paste. The flesh of umeboshi plums is used to make umeboshi plum paste, a creamy purée that is used as a seasoning.

Umeboshi vinegar. Umeboshi vinegar is a salty and sour vinegar made from umeboshi plums.

Wakame. A long, thin, green sea vegetable with a subtle, sweet flavor, wakame is often used in miso soups and salads.

Xanthan gum. Xanthan gum is a substance produced by bacterial fermentation. It is used as an emulsifier, a thickener, and a stabilizer in prepared foods.

Yin and yang. Yin and yang are the two fundamental complementary and antagonistic forces of nature that can be seen in all phenomena. Yang refers to the relative energetic tendencies of contraction, inward and downward movement, density, hardness, gathering, and warmth. Yin refers to the relative energetic tendencies of expansion, outward and upward movement, dispersion, softness, and coolness.

Mail Order Suppliers

With the natural-food movement growing bigger and better every day, it's becoming easier to find wholesome ingredients. Nearly every town has a local natural-food store, and even mainstream grocery stores often carry organic produce and natural foods. Although some of the ingredients called for in the recipes in this book may be hard to find locally, they can be ordered through the companies listed here.

Diamond Organics
www.diamondorganics.com
Diamond Organics delivers organic fresh produce, dry goods, raw foods, and prepared foods from their in-house organic kitchen.

Gold Mine Natural Food Co.
www.goldminenaturalfoods.com
Gold Mine Natural Food Co. offers organic, macrobiotic, vegan, gluten-free, raw, and kosher food selections. They also carry cookware, herbs, and supplements.

Healthy Traders
www.healthytraders.com
Healthy Traders carries a variety of cookware, natural foods, and whole-food supplements.

The Kushi Store
www.kushistore.com
The Kushi Store sells macrobiotic and natural foods, kitchenware, personal care products, and more.

Natural Import Company
www.naturalimport.com
Natural Import Company offers a complete selection of natural Asian foods, including beans, dried fruits, noodles, sea vegetables, and seasonings.

Natural Lifestyle
www.natural-lifestyle.com
Natural Lifestyle carries a wide range of macrobiotic foods and ingredients, as well as cookware, kitchenware, pressure cookers, and rice cookers.

Suggested Reading

Neal Barnard

Eat Right, Live Longer: Using the Natural Powers of Foods to Age-Proof Your Body, Three Rivers Press, 1996.

Dr. Neal Barnard's Program for Reversing Diabetes: The Scientifically Proven System for Reversing Diabetes without Drugs, Rodale Books, 2008.

Edward Esko

Healing Planet Earth: Guidelines for an Ecologically Balanced Diet and Lifestyle, One Peaceful World Press, 1992.

Kathy Freston

Quantum Wellness: A Practical and Spiritual Guide to Health and Happiness, Weinstein Books, 2008.

Rory Freedman and Kim Barnouin

Skinny Bitch: A No-Nonsense, Tough-Love Guide for Savvy Girls Who Want to Stop Eating Crap and Start Looking Fabulous, Running Press, 2005.

Skinny Bitch in the Kitch: Kick-Ass Recipes for Hungry Girls Who Want to Stop Cooking Crap (and Start Looking Hot!), Running Press, 2007.

Skinny Bitch Bun in the Oven: A Gutsy Guide to Becoming One Hot and Healthy Mother!, Running Press, 2008.

Skinny Bastard: A Kick in the Ass for Real Men Who Want to Stop Being Fat and Start Getting Buff, Running Press, 2009.

Michio Kushi with Stephen Blauer

The Macrobiotic Way: The Complete Macrobiotic Lifestyle Book, Avery, 2004.

Michio Kushi and Alex Jack

The Macrobiotic Path to Total Health: A Complete Guide to Naturally Preventing and Relieving More Than 200 Chronic Conditions and Disorders, Ballantine Books, 2004.

Christina Pirello

Cook Your Way to the Life You Want, HP Trade, 2002.

Christina Cooks: Everything You Always Wanted to Know about Whole Foods but Were Afraid to Ask, HP Trade, 2004.

Cooking the Whole Foods Way: Your Complete, Everyday Guide to Healthy, Delicious Eating with 500 Vegan Recipes, Menus, Techniques, Meal Planning, Buying Tips, Wit, and Wisdom, HP Trade, 2007.

Jessica Porter

The Hip Chick's Guide to Macrobiotics: A Philosophy for Achieving a Radiant Mind and a Fabulous Body, Avery Trade, 2004.

Peter Singer and Jim Mason

The Way We Eat: Why Our Food Choices Matter, Rodale Press, 2006.

Kristina Turner

The Self-Healing Cookbook: Whole Foods to Balance Body, Mind and Moods, Earthtones Press, 2002.

Verne Varona

Nature's Cancer-Fighting Foods: Prevent and Reverse the Most Common Forms of Cancer Using the Proven Power of Great Food and Easy Recipes, Reward Books, 2001.

Rebecca Wood

The New Whole Foods Encyclopedia: A Comprehensive Resource for Healthy Eating, Penguin, 2010.

Index

Recipe names appear
in **bold** typeface.

BOOK PUBLISHING COMPANY

since 1974—books that educate, inspire, and empower

To find your favorite vegetarian and soyfood products online, visit:
www.healthy-eating.com

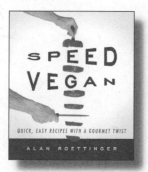

Speed Vegan
Alan Roettinger
978-1-57067-224-6
$19.95

The 4-Ingredient Vegan
Maribeth Abrams
Anne Dinshah
978-1-57067-232-3
$14.95

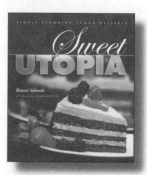

Sweet Utopia
Sharon Valencik
978-1-57067-233-0
$19.95

Local Bounty
Devra Gartenstein
978-1-57067-219-4
$17.95

**The Simple Little
Vegan Slow Cooker**
Michelle Rivera
978-1-57067-251-4
$9.95

Vegan Bites
Beverly Lynn Bennett
978-1-57067-221-7
$15.95

Purchase these health titles and cookbooks from your local bookstore
or natural-food store, or you can buy them directly from:

Book Publishing Company • P.O. Box 99 • Summertown, TN 38483
1-800-695-2241

Please include $3.95 per book for shipping and handling.